"Though little known outside the Stone-Campbell churches of North America, David Lipscomb has exerted profound influence on millions of Christians around the world. This set of essays by a first-rate assemblage of scholars seeks to help us understand an underappreciated aspect of his life, thought, and writings—his political theology, which was prophetic and profound— and apply it critically to our own day and age. It deserves a wide reading, and Lipscomb himself deserves far more attention from students of American religion and public life."

—**Douglas A. Sweeney,** Dean and Professor of Divinity, Beeson Divinity School, Samford University

"In an era in which Libertarians have discovered David Lipscomb, it is critical that those who entertain Lipscomb's religious commitments probe in detail and in-depth the nuances of his 'political' theology. Hicks, Hughes, Goode, Jeffery, and Camp have done just that in an exemplary fashion. They have copiously documented Lipscomb's outlooks on the kingdom of God, government, and race and their relationships, situating them in their twentieth century milieu. They have likewise meticulously surveyed the appropriate scholarship of the past fifty years. Their book provides much food for thought in our current environment. These scholars challenge us to work out how Christians should relate to the government and live in community."

—**Thomas H. Olbricht,** Distinguished Professor Emeritus of Religion, Pepperdine University

"*Resisting Babel* provides a concise introduction to Lipscomb's social and political legacy that is both sympathetic and critical. In so doing, it provides valuable resources for all disciples aspiring to bear faithful witness to the inescapably political gospel of Jesus Christ. Campbellites of all stripes have forgotten why and how to resist the Babels of our day, and if we don't snap out of such amnesia, we'll have little resources for resisting the declining relevance of our churches."

—**John C. Nugent,** author of *Endangered Gospel* and *The Politics of Yahweh,* and cohost of the *After Class* podcast

"This timely book offers an unprecedented historical and theological exploration of the 'apocalyptic' tradition in Churches of Christ—its origins in Barton Stone; its contours in David Lipscomb's thought; its influence on Lipscomb's race relations; its comparison to competing political theologies; its waning in the twentieth century among Churches of Christ; and its usefulness for

Christian thought and practice today. We are indebted to these authors for illuminating how Christians might critically appropriate David Lipscomb's rich political theology to bear faithful witness to the kingdom of God."

—**James L. Gorman,** Associate Professor of History, Johnson University

"Exploring and teasing at the quaint wisdom of David Lipscomb is the prism for a much deeper engagement into the demands of Christian loyalty or allegiance to God. The Churches of Christ once had a chance to choose a different trajectory as they emerged from the Civil War, during which time the warring governments had divided churches and pitted brother against brother, family against family. Churches of Christ, in the main, rejected this chance to disentangle themselves from American politics and pursue the goals of the peaceable kingdom. However, the chaotic and ineffective politics of today's powermongers may create an environment where the way trod by David Lipscomb actually makes sense. These writers push us to ponder the nature of power and the way of discipleship."

—**Stanley N. Helton,** President and Professor of New Testament, Alberta Bible College

"This scrupulously honest book demonstrates in the life of David Lipscomb both the revolutionary social vision of the gospel combined with the example of the early church, and the power of American culture to subvert this vision. Don't just read it and weep. Read it and take stock, then take heed."

—**Shirley Showalter,** author, speaker, and former Professor of English and President of Goshen College

"At a time when many American Christians unquestioningly affirm patriotism, nationalism, and partisan politics as spiritual values, David Lipscomb's voice rings out as one crying in the desert. His radical views on the relationship between Christians and civic government find renewed relevance in today's society. These writers have done a great service to the modern church, better preparing her to engage the current American political system."

—**Timothy Archer,** Director of International Ministry, Herald of Truth, Abilene, Texas

"David Lipscomb was radical before radical was cool. His life shows us that one can be deeply political without being partisan, that one can work for liberation and abhor violence. Lipscomb stood for and with the poor against their rich oppressors, and demanded of Christians that they not kill one another. The writers here show that rather than move with the confusing whims of Babel, Lipscomb stood firm on the Rock of Ages, not building a tower to heaven but bearing witness to the reign of heaven on earth."

—**Justin Bronson Barringer,** coeditor of *A Faith Not Worth Fighting For*

ALLEGIANCE TO GOD
AND THE PROBLEM
OF GOVERNMENT

RESISTING BABEL

EDITED BY

JOHN MARK HICKS

Abilene Christian University Press

RESISTING BABEL
Allegiance to God and the Problem of Government

ACU PRESS

Copyright © 2020 by John Mark Hicks

ISBN 978-1-68426-450-6 | LCCN 2019039408

Printed in the United States of America

LIBRARY OF CONGRESS CATALOGING-IN-PUBLICATION DATA
Names: Hicks, John Mark, 1957- editor.
Title: Resisting Babel : allegiance to God and the problem of government /
    edited by John Mark Hicks.
Description: Abilene, Texas : ACU Press, 2020. | Includes bibliographical references.
Identifiers: LCCN 2019039408 | ISBN 9781684264506 (trade paperback)
Subjects: LCSH: Lipscomb, David, 1831-1917. | Christianity and politics. |
    Christianity and culture.
Classification: LCC BX7343.L56 R47 2020 | DDC 261.7092—dc23
LC record available at https://lccn.loc.gov/2019039408

Cover design by ThinkPen Design
Interior text design by Sandy Armstrong, Strong Design

For information contact:
Abilene Christian University Press
ACU Box 29138
Abilene, Texas 79699

1-877-816-4455
www.acupressbooks.com

20 21 22 23 24 25 / 7 6 5 4 3 2 1

Living in the hope of the moment when the kingdom of the world will "become the kingdom of our Lord and Messiah, and he will reign forever and ever" (Rev. 11:15).

Contents

Introduction

Lipscomb, the War, and the Kingdom Vision

JOHN MARK HICKS

Human government is still Babel—confusion, strife.

—David Lipscomb (1881)

David Lipscomb was arguably the most influential thought leader among Churches of Christ in the United States from the Civil War to the beginning of World War I. He was born in Franklin County, Tennessee, on September 21, 1831; lived almost his whole adult life in Nashville; and died there on September 11, 1917. He edited the leading periodical of Churches of Christ, called the *Gospel Advocate*, from 1866 until his death; cofounded the Nashville Bible School (now Lipscomb University) with James A. Harding in 1891; and conducted revival meetings, planted churches, and preached throughout Middle Tennessee and beyond.

The Civil War was the most traumatic event in the history of the United States, and Lipscomb was in his early thirties at the time. There is little doubt it shifted his thinking in some ways, deepened his convictions in others, and fueled his passion for the kingdom

9

of God. Lipscomb saw the devastating effects of the war in his own personal losses; the death of several cousins, fellow students, and teachers; and the poverty that enveloped Middle Tennessee.

Lipscomb also knew slavery. He became a slave owner in 1853 through inheritance, and he owned five slaves in 1860. In hindsight, Lipscomb saw the Civil War as God's chastening scourge that was necessary for the liberation of African slaves from their southern masters. This, too, shaped Lipscomb's political theology. At some point, Lipscomb came to believe that not only was violence unacceptable for Christians, but any participation in civil affairs that supported coercive political policy was contrary to the spirit of Jesus.

This book intends to identify, contextualize, and understand Lipscomb's political theology. How might contemporary disciples of Jesus draw on his perspectives and experiences as a resource for living in a politically charged present? This project tells the story of a compelling, coherent, and eschatologically grounded vision, which fostered deep and significant religious reform in the United States and led to missionary zeal across the globe. That vision articulated a way forward for Christianity amid the world powers, though it was trumped by those powers and subverted by its own implicit assumptions from within and the overwhelming forces of Babel without. What happened among Churches of Christ serves as a case study, or a parable, of both possibility and warning in the troubling times in which we find ourselves today.

In the first chapter, Richard T. Hughes, a renowned historian of the Stone-Campbell movement, places Lipscomb in the trajectory of Barton W. Stone, who was one of the earliest leaders of what became the Christian Churches, Disciples of Christ, and Churches of Christ. The origins of Lipscomb's apocalyptic theology find their roots in Stone, and they were passed to him through

Tolbert Fanning, Lipscomb's mentor. Hughes provides a backdrop for the development of Lipscomb's own political theology.

In Chapter Two, John Mark Hicks, who has devoted much of his academic career to studying the cofounders of Lipscomb University (David Lipscomb and James A. Harding), expounds Lipscomb's political theology. Lipscomb extends Stone's apocalyptic theology and applies it in the aftermath of the Civil War. At the root of this apocalyptic agenda was his conviction that humanity had transferred its allegiance from the peaceable reign of God to the militant and selfish interests of human governments. Civil government, in Lipscomb's view, had not only subverted the kingdom of God in the mind of most Christians but replaced it.

In the next chapter, Hicks offers a case study of Lipscomb's applied apocalyptic political theology. How does a citizen of the kingdom of God live in a nation where Africans, recently freed from slavery, are struggling to live freely in a hostile and oppressive social environment? The chapter examines Lipscomb's views on slavery, racism, and segregation. Does his apocalyptic theology make any real difference? How does the church practice the reality of the kingdom of God within its own community and within society? Lipscomb, we will see, did not fully escape his own southern sectionalism.

In Chapter Four, Richard C. Goode, a professor of history and political science, maps David Lipscomb onto the larger topography of American religious and political thought. In particular, Lipscomb represents a pilgrim political theology that has historically relegated adherents to the margins so that they become sojourners or resident aliens in and among nation–states and civil governments (foregoing rights, privileges, and powers). As a practitioner of this radical political theology (in contrast to transformationist and realist ones), Lipscomb belongs in a tradition also represented by Adin Ballou, Clarence Jordan, William

Stringfellow, Will Campbell, and Dorothy Day. Consequently, Lipscomb is no lone ranger in his pursuit, but participates in a larger tradition that reaches back at least to the Anabaptists and, as Lipscomb saw it, back to the Christians of the first three centuries.

In Chapter Five, Joshua Ward Jeffery, an authority on pacifism and World War I, explores the decline of pacifism and nonparticipation in civil government among Churches of Christ. The challenge to apocalypticism began during World War I as the US government applied immense pressure to pacifist groups to support the war effort. The slow declension of Lipscomb's view and increased acculturation continued into the interwar years and the World War II era before accelerating during the Cold War.

In the final chapter, Lee C. Camp, a leader in ethical thought within Churches of Christ, reviews and summarizes the heritage of David Lipscomb with an eye toward contemporary relevance and application. Camp raises critical questions—such as, how do we embrace practices of nonviolence without relinquishing a voice for justice and peacemaking in the public square? He assesses the limits (even short-sightedness) of Lipscomb's vision, while also proposing the contemporary fruitfulness of some of his key theological commitments.

The present political climate has awakened interest in Lipscomb's apocalyptic sectarianism in some quarters. Lipscomb's understanding of the kingdom of God, rooted in the Sermon on the Mount, subverts the present Evangelical church, which seems deeply committed to nationalism, patriotism, and political power.

While we may yet engage the political struggle and seek political power, perhaps it might serve us well to listen to Lipscomb once again, if only to temper our efforts with the spirit of Jesus and reorient our vision in the light of the kingdom of God. This does not, of course, mean we fully embrace everything Lipscomb believed, but it does mean we listen carefully to the voice of a

Christ follower who lived through the most tumultuous political period in the history of the United States.

As we enter Lipscomb's world from the Civil War (1861–65) through Reconstruction (1865–77) and into the segregationist Jim Crow era (1877–1964), we listen. We seek to understand his context and commitments, observe his practices, and watch how his voice was silenced by World War I. This work breathes the world of the United States from 1861 to 1918, which are the dates when David Lipscomb was the most significant editor, even editor-bishop, among Churches of Christ. We hope to learn from this history, continue to pursue the kingdom of God, and practice the kingdom in the present. We think Lipscomb might help us do that.

1

"The Politics of the Day" and "The Politics of Heaven"

The Apocalyptic Orientation of Barton W. Stone

RICHARD T. HUGHES

We must return to the government, laws, and ordinances of our rightful king, the Lord Jesus, before we shall be ever gathered together and become worthy subjects of his kingdom. We must unite our energies, advance the government and kingdom of our Lord, and meddle not with the government of this world, whether human, ecclesiastical, or political, or civil; all others aside from that of heaven will be put down by a firm decree of our Lord before the end come.

—Barton W. Stone (1844)

In June of 2018, the attorney general of the United States, Jefferson Beauregard Sessions III, publicly quoted the Bible to defend a strategy of the federal government designed to discourage Latino/a immigrants from entering the United States. Immoral by any measure, that strategy required border agents to separate children from their parents, to criminalize and deport parents guilty of nothing more than seeking asylum, and to place the children in detention camps before sending them to foster homes and adoption agencies throughout the nation. To defend this action against its critics, Sessions marshaled Romans 13:1. "I would cite to you," Sessions said, "the Apostle Paul and his clear and wise command in Romans 13 to obey the laws of the government because God has ordained the government for his purposes."[1]

Conveniently—and ignorantly perhaps as well—Sessions failed to note the strong counterwitness that runs throughout the Bible, calling on God's people to resist human governments when those governments seek to usurp the place of God. For example, every Sunday-school child learns the story of Shadrach, Meshach, and Abednego. When King Nebuchadnezzar commanded that all his subjects fall down and worship, upon pain of death, the golden image he had erected, these three pointedly replied to the king, "We want you to know, Your Majesty, that we will not serve your gods or worship the image of gold you have set up." (Dan. 3:18).

Indeed, according to 1 Samuel 8:6–7—the text upon which David Lipscomb based his book *Civil Government*—the fact that human governments exist at all is an affront to God's sovereign rule. When the ancient Israelites begged God's prophet Samuel for a king "to lead us," God told Samuel, "it is not you they have rejected, but they have rejected me as their king" (1 Sam. 8:6–7).

Of all the biblical texts that summon God's people to resist oppressive and immoral governments that aspire to sit on the throne of God, none is more pointed than the last book in the Bible, the book of Revelation. The message of that book is remarkably similar to the message Shadrach, Meshach, and Abednego delivered to King Nebuchadnezzar: do not worship the king or the empire or conform to the empire's evil decrees. Even if the empire kills you, stand firm and resist until death.

One short verse, in fact, summarizes the message of Revelation: "Do not be afraid of what you are about to suffer. I tell you, the devil will put some of you in prison to test you, and you will suffer persecution for ten days. Be faithful, even to the point of death, and I will give you life as your victor's crown" (Rev. 2:10).

Countercultural Theologians: "The Biblical Topic Is Politics"

Revelation—that inherently seditious book—served in 1973 as the basis for William Stringfellow's now classic-text *An Ethic for Christians and Other Aliens in a Strange Land*, a book that appeared in print just as the Vietnam War was coming to an end and the last American troops were returning home. Here, Stringfellow makes the audacious but profoundly biblical claim that "the biblical topic is politics"[2] and, "except for the accounts of the Crucifixion of Jesus Christ in the Gospels, Revelation is manifestly the most political part of the New Testament."[3]

In light of the political nature of the biblical text, Stringfellow sought in his book "to understand America biblically—*not* the other way around, *not* to construe the Bible Americanly." In light of the moral crisis of the Vietnam War, he viewed his task as urgent, as the nation, along with its churches, had created a

civic religion . . . [that] arrogantly misappropriates political images from the Bible and applies them to America, so that America is conceived of as Zion: as the righteous nation, as a people of superior political morality, as a country and society chosen and especially esteemed by God.[4]

When Stringfellow claimed that "the biblical topic is politics," he did not mean that the Bible endorses one political party against another. He meant something far more radical than that. He wrote:

The Bible is about . . . the politics of the nations, institutions, ideologies, and causes of this world and the politics of the Kingdom of God; the politics of Babylon and the politics of Jerusalem; the politics of the

Antichrist and the politics of Jesus Christ; the politics of
the demonic powers and principalities and the politics
of the timely judgment of God as sovereign; the politics
of death and the politics of life.[5]

Having laid out that premise, he devoted the rest of his book
to explaining how it is that every nation, every imperial power,
including the United States of America, inevitably stands with
the antichrist against Jesus Christ, with the demonic powers
against the sovereignty of God, and with the politics of death
against the politics of life. Even nations that claim to be "Christian
nations"—and here the United States was then, and still is, exhibit
"A"—inevitably resist the kingdom of God and embrace the politics
of death, often disguised as virtue.

The metaphor around which Stringfellow constructed his
book is the very same metaphor that stands at the heart of the
book of Revelation: the metaphor of Babylon. While Revelation
pointedly called upon Christians to resist the godlike pretentions
of the Roman Empire, its author knew that to speak pointedly of
Rome would risk the lives of his readers. He therefore cloaked the
name of Rome with the metaphor of Babylon—an equally brutal
and pretentious regime that had collapsed in the sixth century
BCE. His readers, however, knew exactly what he meant when
they read passages like this one:

Fallen! Fallen is Babylon the Great!
    She has become a dwelling for demons,
and a haunt for every impure spirit,
    a haunt for every unclean bird,
    a haunt for every unclean and detestable animal.
For all nations have drunk
    the maddening wine of her adulteries.

The kings of the earth have committed adultery with her,
    and the merchants of the earth grew rich from
    excessive luxuries. (Rev. 18:2–3)

For those reasons, John charged his readers:

"Come out of her, my people,"
    so that you will not share in her sins,
    so that you will not receive any of her plagues;
for her sins are piled high to heaven,
    and God has remembered her crimes. (Rev. 18:4–5)

After describing Babylon's utter destruction, John then wrote that he "heard what sounded like the roar of a great multitude in heaven shouting":

"Hallelujah!
Salvation and glory and power belong to our God,
    for true and just are his judgments.
He has condemned the great prostitute
    who corrupted the earth by her adulteries.
He has avenged on her the blood of his servants."
And again they shouted:
"Hallelujah!
The smoke from her goes up for ever and ever."
The twenty-four elders and the four living creatures
fell down and worshipped God, who was seated on the
throne. And they cried:
"Amen, Hallelujah!" (Rev. 19:1–4)

The point of this passage should be as clear to us as it was to John's readers: Rome, through its brutal tyranny, has sought to usurp the throne of God, but "salvation and glory and power belong [only] to our God."

But there is more—for in Revelation 21:1–4, John contrasts the blasphemous city of Babylon with the "new Jerusalem":

> Then I saw "a new heaven and a new earth," for the first heaven and the first earth had passed away, and there was no longer any sea. I saw the Holy City, the new Jerusalem, coming down out of heaven from God, prepared as a bride beautifully dressed for her husband. And I heard a loud voice from the throne saying, "Look! God's dwelling place is now among the people, and he will dwell with them. They will be his people, and God himself will be with them and be their God. 'He will wipe away every tear from their eyes. There will be no more death' or mourning or crying or pain, for the old order of things have passed away."

Of the striking contrast John draws between the demonic city of Babylon and the heavenly city of Jerusalem, Stringfellow wrote that "the Babylon epic bespeaks the moral character of *every* nation and of every other principality which is or which was or which may be."[6] In every period of human history,

> Babylon is the city of death, Jerusalem is the city of salvation; Babylon, the dominion of alienation, babel, slavery, war, Jerusalem, the community of reconciliation, sanity, freedom, peace; Babylon, the harlot, Jerusalem, the bride of God; Babylon, the realm of demons and foul spirits, Jerusalem, the dwelling place in which all creatures are fulfilled; Babylon, an abomination to the Lord, Jerusalem, the holy nation; Babylon, doomed, Jerusalem, redeemed.[7]

Having laid that groundwork, Stringfellow made the point that lent his treatise relevance and gave it its cutting edge: "The

Babylon of Revelation is archetypical of all nations."[8] And why? Because of the nature of nations and human governments. Accordingly, Stringfellow wrote:

> Babylon's futility is her idolatry—her boast of . . . moral ultimacy in her destiny, her reputation, her capabilities, her authority, her glory as a nation. The moral pretenses of Imperial Rome, the millennial claims of Nazism, the arrogance of Marxist dogma, the anxious insistence that America be "number one" among nations are all versions of Babylon's idolatry. All share in this grandiose view of the nation by which the principality assumed the place of God in the world.[9]

To Christians who read the Bible through the lens of American culture—both then and now—Stringfellow's argument seems scandalous and preposterous. But to people who read American culture through the lens of the biblical narrative, the truth of Stringfellow's argument seems obvious.

In the United States, there is a community of theologians who have discerned the truth that "the biblical topic is politics," who have read American culture through the lens of the biblical text, and who have understood that the drama played out in that text is the struggle between the kingdoms of this earth and the kingdom of God. William Stringfellow belongs to that community, along with theologians like Walter Wink, James Cone, John Howard Yoder, Kelly Brown Douglas, Stanley Hauerwas, Greg Boyd, and Walter Brueggemann, to name a few.

David Lipscomb

For all his obscurity as a nineteenth-century leader of a small denomination largely confined to four states in the American South—Tennessee, Arkansas, Oklahoma, and Texas—David

Lipscomb (1831–1917) also stands squarely in that community of theologians.

Lipscomb's theology, in fact, anticipated that of Stringfellow when he identified Babylon with human governments—the best along with the worst. "All human government rests for authority upon the power of the sword," Lipscomb wrote. "Its mission has been strife and bloodshed." He thus argued that "to come out of Babylon is to come out of the affiliation and association with human governments. The fall of Babylon is the down fall of all human governments and the destruction of human institutions and authority, and the reinstation of God's rule and authority on earth."[10]

While Lipscomb believed that humankind had usurped God's sovereign right to govern, he also believed that in the final days, God would establish once again his rule over all the earth. When that grand event transpired, God would destroy all human governments—even democracy in the United States. He therefore surmised that "the end of all conflicts and strifes of earth will be the complete and final destruction, the utter consuming of the last vestige of human governments and institutions."[11]

Lipscomb came to this position at some point after 1860, perhaps during the Civil War. In fact, he voted in 1860, casting his ballot for John Bell, the presidential candidate of the Constitutional Union Party.[12] In addition, the 1860 census shows that in that year, Lipscomb owned five people he had enslaved.[13] Clearly, as the war approached, Lipscomb was in many ways a conventional Christian and a conventional citizen of the American South.

The fact that Lipscomb voted in 1860, for a candidate put forward by the Constitutional Union Party is telling. Organized in 1860, that party was committed to one single principle—to avoid secession over slavery. And in light of Lipscomb's later rejection of all human governments as rebellion against the sovereignty of God, it is significant that in 1860, he could vote for a political party whose platform included this resolution: "to recognize no political principle other than THE CONSTITUTION OF THE COUNTRY, THE UNION OF THE STATES, AND THE ENFORCEMENT OF THE LAWS."[14]

Five years before he cast that vote, when Lipscomb was only twenty-four years old, he delivered a speech to the Alumni Association of Franklin College in which he praised the American government as "the first political fruit of Christianity" and argued that "every patriot lover of liberty [should] accept, and jealously preserve inviolable, the franchises of freedom as the gifts of God." He continued, "We would especially have every American free-man approach the ballot box of his country as the sacramental altar of his God—with bared feet and uncovered head, conscious that he treads upon holy ground."[15]

It seems clear that along with influence exerted on Lipscomb by his mentor, Tolbert Fanning, the Civil War was the defining factor that drove Lipscomb to reject all human governments as usurpers of God's rightful rule. By the time the war was over in 1865, Lipscomb was so disillusioned with civil governments that from that time on, he steadfastly refused to vote—a position he held until his death in 1917.

At the same time, he took with absolute seriousness Jesus's command to "love your enemies" from the outset of the war. He rejected carnal warfare as state-sponsored murder, and even when the Civil War engulfed his home town of Nashville, Tennessee, he refused to take sides, risking charges of treason against the Confederate States of America. Several years after the war had ended, he reflected on those calamitous days and the isolation he experienced at the time:

In the beginning of the late strife that so fearfully
desolated our country, much was said about "our
enemies." I protested constantly that I had not a single
enemy, and was not an enemy to a single man North
of the Ohio river. I have never been brought into
collision with one—but very few knew such a person as
myself existed. . . . Yet, these thousands and hundreds
of thousands who knew not each other . . . were made
enemies to each other and thrown into fierce and
bloody strife, were enbued with the spirit of destruction
one toward the other, through the instrumentality of
human governments.[16]

It seems clear that Lipscomb did not arrive at the radical position
he articulated in his book *Civil Government* all at once, but grew
into the fullness of that position, piece by piece, over a period
of years. The first piece was his pacifism, apparently on display
throughout the Civil War. The second piece—his opposition to
human governments—did not emerge until sometime during
that war.

Barton W. Stone

There can be little doubt that Lipscomb learned his lessons about
pacifism and the primacy of the kingdom of God ultimately from
the first-generation leader of the Stone-Campbell movement,
Barton W. Stone, and then from Lipscomb's immediate mentor,
Tolbert Fanning.

Three preachers schooled by Stone—Ephraim D. Moore,
Ross Houston, and James E. Matthews—tutored Fanning in the
Christian faith[17]; and of Moore in particular, Fanning wrote, "We
are more indebted to [him] for our early religious instruction and
impressions than to any other man dead or alive."[18] Indeed, in 1861,

seven months into the Civil War, Fanning confessed, "From our earliest acquaintance with the Sacred Oracles, we have entertained not a doubt that the Church of God is . . . destined, finally, . . . to triumph over all the powers of the earth."[19] In acknowledging his debt to Matthews, it seems clear that Fanning implicitly acknowledged his debt to Stone as well.

The first thing to be said about Stone is that he, too, belonged to that community of American theologians who grasped the truth that "the biblical topic is politics," who read American culture through the lens of the biblical text, and who understood that the drama played out in that text is the struggle between the kingdoms of earth and the kingdom of God.

Like David Lipscomb, Stone did not arrive at those positions all in one fell swoop, but grew into them gradually. What enabled that growth was a biblical principle that lived in Stone's heart at least from his twenty-fifth year—a guiding perspective I once described as his "apocalyptic worldview." That perspective was not the same as a premillennial orientation, but rather an outlook, a cast of mind, that, as I wrote in 1996, "led Stone and many of his followers to act as though the final rule of the kingdom of God were present in the here and now." Indeed, Stone and his people "lived their lives in the shadow of the second coming and thought of themselves as pilgrims who affirmed their allegiance to the kingdom of God rather than to the popular values of the world."[20] Stone's refusal to pledge allegiance to the popular values of the world would, in time, morph into his rejection of human governments as fundamentally antagonistic to the kingdom of God. But rejecting human government as alien to the kingdom of God was not—at least as I understood it in 1996—the essence of the apocalyptic perspective.

The essence, instead, is pledging "allegiance to the kingdom of God rather than to the popular values of the world," and Stone revealed his embrace of that viewpoint at least by 1797, when he was twenty-five years old and visiting Wadmalaw Island and Johns Island in South Carolina. There, he witnessed white, "Christian" slaveholders living in opulence while they terrorized the people they had enslaved. Stone reflected on that scene in his autobiography:

> Before I reached Charleston, I passed over Stone river into John's and Wadmalaw islands. There I remained some days, and received the most friendly attention of gentlemen professing religion, living in splendid palaces, surrounded with a rich profusion of luxuries, and of every thing desirable; these pleasures were heightened by free, humble, and pious conversation. But in the midst of all this glory, my soul sickened at the sight of slavery in more horrid forms than I had ever seen it before; poor negroes! Some chained to their work— some wearing iron collars—all half naked, and followed and driven by the merciless lash of a gentleman overseer—distress appeared scowling in every face.

Then Stone made a telling statement: "This was the exciting cause of my abandonment of slavery."[21]

In addition to his graphic description of the terrors of American slavery, several phrases in this report are especially significant. The first is his statement, "This was the exciting cause of my abandonment of slavery." It is important to note that in turning his back on slavery, he turned his back on the laws of the United States, rejected popular values, and began his embrace of an apocalyptic worldview.

The only way to ignore the apocalyptic dimensions of Stone's theology in 1797 is to ignore—or fail to recognize—two competing realities: (1) Stone's utter commitment to God's rule in his life, already well in place by 1797, and (2) the utter brutality of slavery. What Stone witnessed on those islands forced him to choose between the rule of God on the one hand, and the laws of the United States that sustained American slavery on the other. He clearly chose the kingdom of God, a decision that reflected his already well-developed apocalyptic perspective.

Indeed, in a letter Stone wrote around 1800 to Samuel Rennels, pastor of the Paris, Kentucky, Presbyterian Church, Stone said of slavery: "Christians ought not to let civil policy oppose the express will of God. If we know God's will, we are not to enquire whether it will be [in] our interest to do it."[22]

The second significant phrase in Stone's report is his description of the "gentlemen *professing religion*" (emphasis mine). When Stone contrasted those "gentlemen" who lived "in splendid palaces, surrounded with a rich profusion of luxuries" with the terror those very same gentlemen inflicted on the enslaved people, Stone could only conclude that these individuals were hardly serious Christians—a point he underscored when he used the word "professing."

Stone's comment about the "gentlemen professing religion" leveled a scathing indictment, to be sure. But it was hardly as scathing as some of the comments offered by the black abolitionist Frederick Douglass in a speech he delivered in 1852, eight years after Stone had died. At the very least, Douglass helps us understand the realities of American slavery that made such an impression on Stone in 1797. And he helps us understand those "gentlemen professing religion" and the depravity of significant segments of the American church. Douglass called his speech "What to the Slave Is the Fourth of July?"

> The church of this country is not only indifferent to
> the wrongs of the slave, it actually takes sides with the

oppressors. . . . It is . . . a religion which favors the rich against the poor; which exalts the proud above the humble; which divides mankind into two classes, tyrants and slaves; which says to the man in chains, *stay there,* and to the oppressor, *oppress on*; it is a religion which may be professed and enjoyed by all the robbers and enslavers of mankind; it makes God a respecter of persons, denies his fatherhood of the race, and tramples in the dust the great truth of the brotherhood of man. All this we affirm to be true of the popular church, and the popular worship of our land and nation—a religion, a church, and a worship which, on the authority of inspired wisdom, we pronounce to be an abomination in the sight of God.[23]

It is therefore little wonder that Stone viewed much of what passed for Christianity in the United States as little more than a sham, especially when compared with the standard of the kingdom of God, whose citizens, according to Scripture, fed the hungry, clothed the naked, and gave the thirsty something to drink (Matt. 25). That commitment helps explain, at least in part, why Stone resigned from his ministry in two Presbyterian congregations in 1803, in order "that my labors should henceforth be directed to advance the Redeemer's kingdom, irrespective of party."

Traditionally, historians have used Stone's phrase "irrespective of party" to argue that his rejection of sectarianism was the driving force behind his departure from the Presbyterian ministry. And while that is true, his commitment to the kingdom of God was a driving force as well, even though that commitment meant a life of poverty. In truth, Stone connected his rejection of sectarianism with his rejection of slavery:

Thus to the cause of truth I sacrificed the friendship of two large congregations, and an abundant salary

for the support of myself and family. I preferred the
truth to the friendship and kindness of my associates
in the Presbyterian ministry, who were dear to me, and
tenderly united in the bonds of love. I preferred honesty
and a good conscience to all these things. Having
now no support from the congregations, and having
emancipated my slaves, I turned my attention cheerfully,
though awkwardly, to labor on my little farm. Though
fatigued in body, my mind was happy, and "calm as
summer evenings be." I relaxed not in my ministerial
labors, preaching almost every night, and often in the
day time, to the people around. I had no money to hire
laborers, and often on my return home, I found the
weeds were getting ahead of my corn. I had often to
labor at night while others were asleep, to redeem my
lost time.[24]

Stone's linking his rejection of sectarianism with his rejection of
slavery was not uncommon for many who participated in the
great Cane Ridge Revival. Newell Williams reports that "the
Presbyterian ministers who supported the revival were, like Stone,
staunch emancipationists."[25] Stone affirmed that "this revival cut
the bonds of many poor slaves"—a fact corroborated, according
to Williams, by the records of Bourbon County where the Cane
Ridge Revival took place. Indeed, during this time, Stone freed a
man and a woman whom he had enslaved and, in so doing, joined
other members of the Cane Ridge Church who, together, filed
twenty-nine deeds of manumission between 1801 and 1819.[26]

The centrality of the commitment of Stone and his followers
to enslaved people is reflected in the autobiography of Joseph
Thomas, a North Carolinian who visited the Stoneite communities
in Kentucky in 1810–11:

> The Christian companies in this settlement and about
> Cane Ridge have been large; but within a few years,
> many of them, who held black people as slaves, emanci-
> pated them, and have moved to the state of Ohio. I will
> observe that the Christians of these parts *abhor* the idea
> of *slavery*, and some of them have almost tho't that they
> who hold to slavery cannot be a Christian.[27]

Stone's commitment to free enslaved people was a constant theme in his career. In 1827, Stone threw his weight behind the work of the American Colonization Society and even called on Congress to help fund that project, designed to return "free People of Colour" to the African colony of Liberia.[28]

Stone's reliance on a human government to achieve that objective, however, in no way means that he had not yet embraced an apocalyptic perspective, as Williams suggests.[29] It means, instead, that Stone was so passionate, so completely dedicated in his commitment to free enslaved people—a commitment that reflected his apocalyptic orientation—that he was willing to utilize human government to accomplish that end.

By 1835, Stone's passion to abolish slavery led him to reprint in his *Christian Messenger* a statement on slavery by a man considered radical in both the North and the South. That man was William Lloyd Garrison, and his statement was his "Address to the People of the United States on Slavery." Garrison called for the *immediate* abolition of slavery, something to which Stone could assent but with which most southern whites, including most southern white Christians, would never agree. And because of threats of violence against abolitionists, presumably including himself, he discontinued publication of Garrison's "Address" after only three installments.

It is worth noting, however, that Stone prefaced the first installment of Garrison's "Address" with a statement of his own conviction: "I have long viewed Slavery as the darkest cloud that hangs over America."[30] Indeed, he had—ever since 1797 when he witnessed the terror inflicted on enslaved people by those "gentlemen professing religion" but "living in splendid palaces."

By 1842, as Williams notes, Stone had lost faith in the American government; and with that turn of mind, his apocalyptic orientation reached new heights. No longer did he simply seek to live his life *as if* God's sovereignty over all the earth and the rule of the kingdom of God were fully present in his own time and place. Now he pledged his exclusive allegiance to the kingdom of God and withdrew his allegiance from the government of the United States.

As Williams shows, he lost faith in the American government, first, because politics in the United States had taken on such highly partisan dimensions. But he also lost faith because of the failure of the American government to banish slavery.[31] Accordingly, in an 1843 essay that Stone appropriately titled "Reflections of Old Age," he asked these probing questions:

> Must we conclude . . . that our Congress and State
> legislatures, are schools of corruption and demoraliza-
> tion?—that the departments of state are nurseries of
> vice and irreligion?—and that the politics of the day are
> in opposition to the politics of heaven?—Dreadful con-
> clusion! Yet how can we evade it . . . ?[32]

A year later, in 1844, Stone composed a fictitious conversation between an old preacher and a young preacher, where the older character says:

We must return to the government, laws and ordinances
of our rightful king, the Lord Jesus, before we shall be
ever gathered together and become worthy subjects of
his kingdom. We must unite our energies, advance the
government and kingdom of our Lord, and meddle
not with the government of this world, whether human,
ecclesiastical, or political, or civil; all others aside from
that of heaven will be put down by a firm decree of our
Lord before the end come.

To that radical statement, the young preacher appealed to the
very passage that the Attorney General of the United States would
employ some 175 years later to justify the intimidation of refugees by separating children from their parents—Romans 13:1: "Let
every person be subject to the governing authorities" (ESV).

"You astonish me," the young preacher said. "Are not the civil
powers and governments that be, ordained of God? And is it not
the duty of Christians to be subject to them, and to sustain them?"

To that question, the old preacher—clearly, Barton W. Stone
himself—had given much thought:

If it be the duty of Christians under one worldly
government to uphold and support that government,
then it is the duty of Christians living in every worldly
government to uphold and support that government;
those living in N. America must uphold and support the
[slaveholding] democracy of the United States; those in
Britain, must support the monarchy of England; those
in Russia, must support the despotism there; those at
Rome, most [sic] support the government of the pope,
the man of sin, the antichrist of our rightful Lord;—
those in South America must support every petty tyrant
that wades through blood to sit in the supreme chair of

state. . . . Can we for one moment think that the Lord enjoined on his people under the Cesars [sic] of old to uphold and defend their bloody governments, which enjoined the extirpation of the Christians, or to force them to abandon their religions and sacrifice to idols?[33]

Stone's conclusion came in the form of two rhetorical questions and then a resounding answer: "Must we be subject to all these powers, never resist them, but always obey them? Did the Apostles resist the higher powers when they were forbidden to teach in the name of Jesus? Nay—they chose to obey God rather than man."[34]

By embracing that conclusion, Stone tapped into that great counternarrative in the biblical text that summons Christians to resist imperial powers that seek to usurp the throne of God. And he took his place in that community of American theologians who, throughout the history of the American nation, have grasped the truth that "the biblical topic is politics," who have read American culture through the lens of the biblical text, and who have under-stood—and still understand—that the drama played out in that text is the struggle between the kingdoms of earth and the king-dom of God.

NOTES

[1] Julie Zauzmer and Keith McMillan, "Sessions Cites Bible Passage Used to Defend Slavery in Defense of Separating Immigrant Families," *Washington Post*, June 15, 2018, https://www.washingtonpost.com/news/acts-of-faith/wp/2018/06/14/jeff-sessions-points-to-the-bible-in-defense-of-separating-immigrant-families/?utm_term=.e2585e730793.

[2] William Stringfellow, *An Ethic for Christians and Other Aliens in a Strange Land* (Eugene, OR: Wipf and Stock, 2004 [1973]), 14.

[3] Stringfellow, *Ethic*, 27.

[4] Stringfellow, *Ethic*, 13–14.

[5] Stringfellow, *Ethic*, 14–15.

[6] Stringfellow, *Ethic*, 33.

[7] Stringfellow, *Ethic*, 34.

[8] Stringfellow, *Ethic*, 48.

[9] Stringfellow, *Ethic*, 51.

[10] David Lipscomb, "Babylon," *Gospel Advocate* 23, no. 22 (June 2, 1881): 340.

[11] Lipscomb, *Civil Government: Its Origin, Mission and Destiny, and the Christian's Relation to It* (Nashville: Gospel Advocate, 1889), 27; cf. also pages 25, 28, 83–88, 96.

[12] Lipscomb, "Our Positions," *Gospel Advocate* 54, no. 34 (August 22, 1912): 954.

[13] US Bureau of Census, Eighth Census of the United States: 1860, Tennessee, Schedule 2, Slave.

[14] Gerhard Peters and John T. Woolley, "Minor/Third Party Platforms, Constitutional Union Party Platform of 1860," The American Presidency Project, https://www.presidency.ucsb.edu/node/273159 (emphasis in the original).

[15] Lipscomb, *The Religious Sentiment: Its Social and Political Influence* (Nashville: Cameron & Fall, 1855), 26, 34, https://webfiles.acu.edu/departments/Library/HR/restmov_nov11/www.mun.ca/rels/restmov/texts/dlipscomb/1855.html.

[16] Lipscomb, "Babylon," *Gospel Advocate* 33, no. 22 (June 2, 1881): 340.

[17] James Wilburn, *The Hazard of the Die: Tolbert Fanning and the Restoration Movement* (Malibu: Pepperdine University Press, 1980), 13–16.

[18] Tolbert Fanning, "Obituary," *Gospel Advocate* 6, no. 1 (January 1860): 31.

[19] Fanning, "Ministers of Peace in the World's Conflicts," *Gospel Advocate* 7, no. 11 (November 1861): 347–48.

[20] I have borrowed this pregnant and highly descriptive phrase from Timothy P. Weber, *Living in the Shadow of the Second Coming: American Premillennialism, 1875–1925* (New York: Oxford University Press, 1979). See also Richard T. Hughes, *Reviving the Ancient Faith: The Story of Churches of Christ in America* (Grand Rapids, MI: Eerdmans, 1996; repr., Abilene, TX: Abilene Christian University Press, 2008), 92–93.

[21] Barton W. Stone, "A Short History of the Life of Barton W. Stone, Written by Himself" (Cincinnati: J. A. & U. P. James, 1847), in *The Cane Ridge Reader*, ed. Hoke S. Dickinson (Cane Ridge, KY: Cane Ridge Preservation Project, 1972), 27–28.

[22] B. W. Stone to Samuel Rennels, Cane Ridge Preservation Project Museum, Cane Ridge, Kentucky, n.d., cited in Newell Williams, "Pursuit of Justice: The Antislavery Pilgrimage of Barton W. Stone," *Encounter* 62, no. 4 (2001): 5. This essay is an excellent account of Stone's antislavery attitudes and activities.

[23] Frederick Douglass, "What, to the Slave, Is the Fourth of July?" in *Lift Every Voice: African American Oratory, 1787–1900*, ed. Philip S. Foner and Robert James Branham (Tuscaloosa: University of Alabama Press, 1998), 262–63.

[24] Stone, "A Short History," 50.

[25] Williams, "Pursuit of Justice," 6; see also Williams, *Barton Stone: A Spiritual Biography* (St. Louis: Chalice Press, 2000), 65–78.

[26] Williams, "Pursuit of Justice," 6–7, and especially n. 14.

[27] Joseph Thomas, *The Travels and Gospel Labors of Joseph Thomas* (Winchester, VA: n.p., 1812), 56.

[28] Stone, "The Honorable the Senate and House of Representatives of the United States in Congress Assembled," *Christian Messenger* 1, no. 8 (June 1827): 180–81.

[29] Williams, "From Trusting Congress to Renouncing Human Governments: The Millennial Odyssey of Barton W. Stone," *Discipliana* 61, no. 3 (September 2001): 67–81. This is an extraordinarily helpful essay that chronicles the sequence of Stone's development. Here, Williams rightly argues that not until 1842 would Stone formally renounce the American political system, along with human governments in every form, and pledge his allegiance instead to the kingdom of God (see especially pages 73–77). Williams concludes, however, that Stone did not embrace an apocalyptic worldview until the 1840s, in part because Williams identifies the apocalyptic perspective with renunciation of human governments. The apocalyptic perspective, however, was far broader than that. In 1992, I suggested that the apocalyptic worldview embraced "a radical sense of estrangement and separation from the world and its values and a keen allegiance to a transcendent vision these people described as 'the Kingdom of God.'" ("The Apocalyptic Origins of Churches of Christ and the Triumph of Modernism," *Religion and American Culture: A Journal of Interpretation* 2, no. 2 [Summer 1992]: 182). Four years later, in my history of Churches of Christ, I tried to broaden that definition, to define the apocalyptic vision in a way that clearly would transcend any single issue, to make clear that the apocalyptic perspective was an orientation of one's life—not an affirmation of a single position or point of view. Thus the term *apocalyptic worldview* "signifies an outlook that led Stone and many of his followers to act as though the final rule of the kingdom of God were present in the here and now. . . . He and many of his coworkers lived their lives in the shadow of the second coming and thought of themselves as pilgrims who affirmed their allegiance to the kingdom of God rather than to the popular values of the world." (*Reviving the Ancient Faith*, 92–93). Williams based his critique only on the more restrictive definition that appeared in the 1992 essay, referencing the 1996 book only in a single footnote.

[30] Stone, comments preceding William Lloyd Garrison, "Address to the People of the United States on Slavery," *Christian Messenger* 9, no. 4 (April 1835): 82.

[31] Williams, "From Trusting Congress," 73.

[32] Stone, "Reflections of Old Age," *Christian Messenger* 13, no. 4 (August 1843): 123.

[33] Stone, "An Interview between an Old and Young Preacher," *Christian Messenger* 14, no. 8 (December 1844): 227–28.

[34] Stone, "Reply to T. P. Ware," *Christian Messenger* 14, no. 6 (October 1844): 169–70.

2

David Lipscomb's Political Theology
Submit but Don't Support

JOHN MARK HICKS

Christ's mission—the mission of his kingdom—is to put down and destroy all these kingdoms, and to destroy everything that exercises rule, authority, or power on earth. How can the servants of Christ and the subjects of his kingdom enter into, strengthen, and build up that which Christ and his kingdom are commissioned to destroy?

—David Lipscomb (1913)

Tolbert Fanning, who baptized David Lipscomb in 1845, educated him at Franklin College from 1845 to 1849, and invited him to coedit the *Gospel Advocate* in 1866, espoused a provocative mix of Barton W. Stone's apocalypticism and Alexander Campbell's primitivism.[1] North Alabama preachers, influenced by Stone, baptized and mentored Fanning, and he accompanied Alexander Campbell on several preaching tours in the 1830s. No other person casts a longer shadow over the Stone-Campbell movement in Middle Tennessee than Fanning in the 1840s–1860s.

Tennessee was a prounion state. It voted for John Bell in the 1860 presidential election, and it voted against secession in February 1861 by a four to one margin. That changed when Abraham Lincoln called for seventy-five thousand volunteers. The state then voted for secession on June 8 and entered the war.

Tolbert Fanning flooded the July 1861 issue of the *Gospel Advocate* with three substantial articles on war, peace, and "world powers."[2] Fanning's lead piece summarized his political theology in five points:[3]

1. God is "sovereign" over the nations, overturning their self-interested acts to God's good purposes.
2. God reigns over the saints through King Jesus, who is tasked with the mission to "subdue the nations."
3. The kingdom of God, which "consists of righteousness, joy and peace in the Holy Spirit," reigns through nonviolence.
4. The kingdom of God stands opposed to "*the world power*" or "*principalities*" and will ultimately triumph over them.
5. The kingdom of God will triumph through nonviolent means as citizens of the kingdom of God, though obedient to human institutions as far as possible, refuse to form alliances with them and thereby leaven the earth with peace and righteousness.

For those acquainted with Fanning, this was no surprise. He had avoided "partisan politics or war" since the early 1840s.[4] Significantly, these five points also effectively summarized Lipscomb's *Civil Government*.[5] But this had not always been Lipscomb's stance.

David Lipscomb in Context

On July 4, 1855, Lipscomb delivered a lecture at the Alumni Society of Franklin College in which he articulated his admiration for the

American political experiment. "Civil government," he said, "is the child of religious faith," and "it is the duty of religion, working through individual faith, to guide, guard, and foster the civil institutions to a free and vigorous growth." Consequently, "every American [should] approach the ballot box of his country as the sacramental altar of his God—with bared feet and uncovered head, conscious that he treads upon holy ground."[6] However, over the next "ten years," Lipscomb later recalled, he attempted to free himself from all political sympathies or antipathies, and he found it "very difficult" to do so because he had allowed himself "to become engrossed in feeling with such affairs."[7]

This shift began when Lipscomb started preaching regularly in 1857.[8] Apparently, the growing war clouds generated a more radical perspective about the relationship of the kingdom of God to civil government. In 1887, he remembered that he had been teaching his settled view for thirty years; and in 1908, wrote it had been fifty years.[9] We can imagine heated debates and the likelihood of war provided a moment of reassessment, and Lipscomb, however slowly, came to adopt Fanning's views.

While Fanning last voted in the 1840s,[10] Lipscomb voted for the Unionist John Bell in 1860.[11] We may surmise the vote was intended to avert secession ("I was not a secessionist"[12]) and war. "We found it difficult to keep out of the late strife," Lipscomb later wrote.[13] Perhaps that vote was a final effort to engage the political process in the hopes of a good outcome. But secession and war came, nevertheless.

At the same time Fanning was opposing political strife and war in the 1861 *Gospel Advocate*, Lipscomb was preaching against such throughout Middle Tennessee. "My friends," Lipscomb wrote, "though I endangered my life in so doing," and on at least one occasion a man, "after I had preached, proposed, if twelve men would join him, they would hang me."[14] Both Unionist and

Confederate partisans regularly "insulted" Lipscomb and regarded him as "disloyal." Yet, as Lipscomb saw it, the "religious bigots" were the real problem, because they were "wholly occupied with the empire of the prince of this world" through their political warmongerings.[15]

At the outbreak of hostilities, Lipscomb "preached and wrote to brethren," to practice the "unity that the Church of Christ should be able to maintain in the face of national difficulties," and for such he suffered reproach and repeated violent threats.[16] Lipscomb, Fanning, and others were able to gather a group of "elders and evangelists" from "ten or fifteen congregations" in Middle Tennessee to petition President Jefferson Davis for exemption from Confederate military service and ultimately presented a similar letter to the Federal governor of Tennessee, Andrew Johnson. Both petitions were successful.[17] Middle Tennessee, according to Lipscomb, was "almost a unit" on this subject.[18]

The documents expressed Fanning's political theology. For example, the letter to the Confederacy rejected "active participation" in processes that "destroy or upbuild" political institutions. The Federal letter is even more explicit: "The spirit of the Church of Christ and the spirit of civil government are different." Further, the petitioners refused to take "oaths of allegiance" because such oaths sanctioned violence.[19]

After the war in 1866, Fanning and Lipscomb restarted the *Gospel Advocate*, which had ceased publication at the end of 1861. A fundamental purpose of the *Gospel Advocate* was to encourage submission "to the decision of Providence" and "accept it as a divine call to find labor and honor in a *higher, holier, heavenly nationality*."[20] They sought "to avoid the utterance of a single political thought" while, at the same time, advocating for a different polis: the kingdom God.[21] To that end, the early years of the *Gospel Advocate* are filled with essays on the relation of the Christian to the civil government, including eighteen essays entitled "The Church of Christ and World Powers," which became the basis of *Civil Government*.[22] Throughout his editorship, Lipscomb regularly published essays on the topic and responded to questions.

Fanning and Lipscomb discovered "sectionalists and politicians North and South," who only "a few short months [ago] were thirsting for each other's blood," were now united "in opposition to us."[23] They were not surprised because they already believed political power was more "intoxicating" than "alcohol and opium."[24]

"Who Shall Govern the World?"

On Christmas Day in 1866, Lipscomb posed this deeply theological question, and its answer lies at the root of how one lives in the world.[25] Lipscomb, and Fanning before him,[26] identified three historic answers:[27]

1. *Institutional* ("Roman Catholic"): "The Church should form alliances with the world institutions, for the purpose of controlling and using those institutions for the advancement of its own interest."

2. *Two kingdoms* ("Protestant"): "Political governments are of Divine origin, as such must be supported and sustained, for their own intrinsic worth, and because they are essential to the well being not only of the world, but the Church itself."

3. *Conflicting kingdoms* (Anabaptist/Mennonite): "Two institutions, the Christian and the worldly, were necessarily separate and distinct. That they could form no alliances. That each was necessary in its proper place and for its proper subjects."

While Lipscomb, along with much of Protestant America, was alarmed by the potential prospects of the first, the second contributed to the origins of the Civil War. When Christians believe it is the "duty and privilege of Christians to actively participate in the governments of the world," then they will "vote, hold office, take the sword and musket and shed the blood of their fellowman, and even brother Christian." This constitutes an "adulterous alliance" between civil power and the kingdom of God.[28]

For Lipscomb, "the two are essentially antagonistic."[29] Each has their role, but "*they must forever remain distinct.*"[30] They are mutually exclusive because the origins and spirit of each are radically different. The two cities, a divine polis and a human polis, are in perpetual conflict.

This conflict is not between heaven and earth, per se, but between *two kingdoms on the earth* that seek sovereignty over the earth and the hearts of the people upon the earth. Both kingdoms are earthy—that is, they exist upon the earth in order to rule the earth. The contrast lies in their origins, missions, weapons, spirits, and destinies.[31]

Consequently, the question of "who governs" is really a question about allegiance or worship. "The Christian," according to Lipscomb, "owes no allegiance" to the civil powers but only "to God."[32] Just as Jesus responded to Satan's offer of the kingdoms of this world, so the Christian must respond: "Worship the Lord your God, and serve him only" (Matt. 4:10). The question "Who shall govern the world?" is more fundamentally the question "Whom shall we worship?"

The kingdom of God began with creation. God gave humanity dominion over the creation but retained the right of sole rule over humanity. God exercised this rule through families, then through the tribal clan of Abraham as a specific family upon the earth, then through the nation of Israel, and then finally through Jesus the Messiah, whose reign is universal and inclusive of all peoples.[33]

However, humanity did not submit to this reign. Through their disobedience, Adam and Eve "transferred the government of the world from God to the evil one."[34] The devil pursued his reign through violence as Cain killed Abel, and the Noahic world was thrown into disarray. Though cleansed by the flood, renewed violence created the first "empire"—Babel, or Babylon. Babylon is the primary symbol of the "world powers" in the biblical narrative, and it epitomizes the "confusion, strife, bloodshed, and perpetual warfare in the world" that arises from the exercise of imperial power.[35]

God permits the rise of "world powers" in order to place boundaries on evil, punish it, and create space for the pursuit of righteousness. In this sense, civil government is "essential" for human flourishing "in the present condition of the world."[36] It is "necessary" for curtailing and punishing evil, and consequently, civil government has its legitimate and "good" role within God's providence.[37] At the same time, it is only necessary due to the presence of evil. God permits Satan to rule over humanity through civil powers but also overrules those powers for God's own purposes.

As human imperial powers rose, God located the divine rule in Abraham's descendants as a nation in contrast to the world powers. Israel, as a nation living under the reign of God, "was the type, not of the political governments of the world, but of the Church of Jesus Christ."[38]

Like Babel, however, Israel desired a "human polity" in place of the God-given theocracy (1 Sam. 8). God granted their request, and thus human polity within Israel was "an ordinance of God" by divine permission.[39] The Israelite experiment in human government ultimately collapsed. What Israel thought was an advance in their civilization, God permitted as an example of disordered desires and their deleterious effects. As Lipscomb continually stressed, God gave Israel a king in divine anger (quoting Hosea 13:9–11).[40]

As Israel's experiment with human polity faltered, God sent Jesus, the true King of Israel, "into this world to re-establish the reign, dominion, kingdom of God on earth in its perfected and final form."[41] In so doing, God began the fulfillment of the prophetic message from Isaiah to Daniel, which promised the destruction of the kingdoms of the earth and the restoration of the kingdom of God.

> The life of Christ was a continual conflict with the rulers of the world. The civil power sought his life at his birth, desolated the homes of Bethlehem by the slaughter of "every male child two year old and under," dogged his pathway through life, arrested him, nailed him to the cross, murdered him, sealed his tomb, and set a watch to prevent his rising. In the dark dungeon of the grave, betrayed of men, forsaken of God (within the personal domain and power of the devil), bound in the fetters of death, he makes the final struggle with "him that hath the power of death, that is the devil." In the grave the final battle was fought. Jesus overcame the devil in his own home, triumphed over death, hell and the grave.[42]

The epitome of this struggle was his confrontation with Satan in the wilderness. The prince of this world offered Jesus royal status with power and wealth. Jesus was tempted to "rule the earth through the devil's kingdoms, without suffering, without death, without the grave."[43] Jesus resisted and recognized the temptation was about loyalty, allegiance, and worship.

The life and ministry of Jesus upon the earth is "a type of the existence of the spiritual body," the church.[44] Consequently, it is no surprise Satan offers the church the same temptation of power and wealth through civil powers, and persecutes the church (as he did the Messiah) through the kingdoms of the earth when it rejects the temptation. The book of Revelation narrates "their opposition to and persecution of the witnesses and worshippers of God."[45]

Two different "spirits" pervade the world powers and the kingdom of God. Each has its "own peculiar spirit that abides in it and animates each of its members." The spirit of the evil one animates civil powers, and this moves humanity to "strife and bloodshed" as the world powers live by the "strength and skill of carnal weapons." Their banners are "drenched in the blood of their enemies shed for their own benefit."[46] "Every human government," Lipscomb wrote, "uses the substance, the time, the service of the subjects to enrich, gratify the appetites and lusts, and to promote the grandeur and glory of its ruler."[47] In contrast,

> God, through his gentle, meek, loving, self-sacrificing
> Son established the Church of Christ, and imparted to
> it his spirit to dwell in, animate, guide, and control that
> body and every member thereof. Whoever puts himself
> under the guidance or control of a different spirit ceases
> to be a member of the Church or body of Christ.

The banner of Jesus the Messiah is the "cross," which "glories in the death of its own subjects for the good of its enemies; its virtue is derived from the bloodstains of its own great standard-bearer, dying that his enemies might live."[48]

For Lipscomb, the Sermon on the Mount "is the moral code of the Christian dispensation"[49] and contains the "great principles" of the kingdom of God. In particular, "his subjects shall not return evil for evil, but they shall return good for evil." One cannot be a "child of God without cultivating and continually practicing this spirit."[50] This is a different spirit from the kingdoms of this world, who must, in order to exist, return evil for evil. The Sermon on the Mount is "diametrically opposed to the principles necessary to the existence of human government," and no one can serve two masters. When the Sermon on the Mount is modified in order to make room for civil powers, one displaces "the Spirit of God that dwells in [God's] institutions with the rebellious spirit of man."[51]

The church is the divine institution commissioned to practice the kingdom of God upon the earth. Civil power can never serve the mission of Jesus because it does not have a suitable spirit. When Christians participate in world powers, they "drink in another spirit" distinct from the "Spirit of God," and they "will bring that spirit into the church of God to secularize and demoralize it," such that the church becomes ineffective in its work.[52] Consequently, any "dependence upon civil government for help or success in this work is treason."[53]

But are not human governments "ordained" of God, according to Romans 13? Lipscomb agreed. Human governments are ordained as servants of God for the punishment of evildoers, just as Assyria and Babylon were ordained to punish Israel and Judah for their sins. Nebuchadnezzar and Nero were "servants of God" in this sense, but no Christian can serve as they served because Romans 12 forbids disciples of Jesus to participate in acts of vengeance and strife. Christians do not return evil for evil but give a cup of cold water to their enemies.[54]

Lipscomb believed the church of the first three centuries pursued this course, and it was only when Constantine wedded the church to the state that Christians began to invest their energies in political processes. Using the historians available to him (Mosheim, Neander, Gibbon, Orchard, Jones), Lipscomb regularly appealed to the nonpolitical and oppressed conditions of the early church.[55] They did not separate themselves from the empire because of their privileged status; they were not privileged people.

Rather, they separated themselves because they recognized the empire as the servant of the evil one.

History is the story of the conflict between these two kingdoms, these two cities. They are essentially antagonistic. They serve different masters, imbibe different spirits, use different weapons, and one must come to an end for the other to fill the earth. And "when Jesus returns again to earth," the "will of God will be done on earth as it is heaven" and everything in the creation will "be restored to harmonious relations with God, the Supreme Ruler of the universe."[56] In that moment, "the atmosphere will be purified of its rebellious taint and death will be destroyed—this world will become an Eden of happiness and peace," and God will once again say, "It is very good."[57]

Living among the World Powers

Given this inherent antagonism between the kingdom of God and world powers, how does one live in the world without imbibing its spirit? What relationship should Christians have with the powers? Lipscomb's response, succinctly stated, is "a submission, not support, is what is required."[58]

This submission is theologically driven. It is not shaped by the civil powers themselves or their inherent worth. Since Christians owe no allegiance to any human government, they do not owe it any obedience due to "any virtue or merit it possesses, but [only] as a solemn duty" owed to God.[59] This obligation is rooted in the greatest command to love God, and this love "limits and modifies all" relationships and "is limited and modified by none." This is the Christian's *sole* allegiance. Whenever Christians submit to civil power, their obedience is shaped by God's values rather than by the state's interests. This submission is "imperative, under all circumstances, to any government, power, or principality, under which we are placed." Whatever "our conceptions of the right or wrong of the government, its justice or injustice, its constitutionality or unconstitutionality, its good or evil tendency," these "neither weaken or strengthen the obligations we owe it," *because it is a duty we owe to God.*[60]

As long as the civil power does not require anything contrary to God's values, the Christian offers "cheerful submission," because God does have good purposes for permitting human governments.[61] The civil power, for example, "is ordained of God for the punishment of evil doers."[62] Consequently, "human government is needful, so long as a considerable portion of the human family" refuses "obedience to God."[63]

Further, there is a relative sense in which "human government is good."[64] It is ordained to provide protected space for human flourishing through the spread of the gospel. To this end, Christians pray for such space. They do not pray for "the ruler's prosperity" or the government's "strength and power," but that Christians might "lead a quiet and peaceable life."[65] Within this protected space, a Christian is, Lipscomb affirms, "a citizen of the human government under which [one] lives."[66] As a citizen living submissively among the world powers, the Christian is entitled to all the rights and protections granted by the government's own decision. Paul, for example, appealed to Caesar for protection, and this is a proper function of government.[67] And this extends to the use of government—as granted by the government—to conduct business, collect debts, and use the court system to settle differences.[68] In this sense, government is good insofar as the government conforms to the divine purposes for which it was ordained.

This submission, however, is always passive; believers do not "support or sustain" the government, but quietly submit.[69] This entails no active participation in the processes or administration of power, because the spirit of civil power is coercive and violent. "Voting and holding office" participate in the "direction and controlling of the powers," and these powers are essentially violent.[70] "Force is the ground-work of all human government," and "no vote" has any "weight unless it is backed by a bullet."[71]

Active participation in the civil power sanctions the use of violence because "civil government is the embodiment of carnal force."[72] Moreover, its spirit is one of "war, strife, [and] self-aggrandizement at the cost of others" that keeps nations in "perpetual war for the purpose of possessing the power and riches of the world." It is a "spirit of self-interest and retaliation," and that spirit is "diametrically opposed to the spirit of Christ and his kingdom."[73] "We have seen," Lipscomb wrote, "the fruits of strife, bitterness, wrath" that come from active participation in civil powers, and "we have seen" churches divided, people murdered, families impoverished, women raped, and fellow Christians seeking the "other's life with the fierceness of a blood-hound."[74] That is not the fruit of God's Spirit.

As long as Christians do not support the government in the sense of controlling or administering its power, they may serve as employees—for example, teaching public school, surveying, or working on a construction contract. In general, one may "work as an employee of the government but not be an officer or supporter."[75] In other words, the Christian cannot create or enforce policy, but can serve in various capacities that do not partake of the civil power's spirit.

But is not paying taxes a form of support? Lipscomb considered it submission to God's command. Paying taxes "imposed by civil authority is a duty" one "owes to Christ." The example of Jesus and apostolic teaching render this obligation unequivocal. Lipscomb surmises this is true, in part, because the government could compel taxation through confiscation, and thus it is better for good order to peacefully submit to such regulations.[76] Lipscomb's own experience confirms this, since he lost his livestock and other property through Confederate and Federal confiscations during the war.[77]

If paying taxes is a sanctioned form of participation, might there be other forms that are not explicitly sanctioned in Scripture? Lipscomb's response betrays a hermeneutical assumption: "God has forbidden his servants to add anything to the things he has ordained."[78] Scripture is sufficient, and other sources do not offer "one word of direction or guidance" about how Christians might actively support human governments.[79] Where there is no direction, it is presumptive to act otherwise, as "God has given no direction to Christians" other than pray and pay taxes.[80] Consequently, "quiet submission" is the "limit and bound" of a Christian's responsibility to the civil power.[81]

Believers submit to the regulations imposed by civil powers, but they do not support its advancement or power. However, when the values and practices of the government are contrary to the ethics of the kingdom, how should a Christian respond? Should a Christian comply with an evil or unjust government? According to Lipscomb, all human governments are evil, and they are constantly engaged in unjust practices, such as the use of violence and the pursuit of war. Nevertheless, Christians obey the requirements imposed by the government unless believers themselves are required to act unjustly or commit evil. In such cases, believers must resist the government and refuse to comply with its requirements.

However, this resistance is nonviolent. It is a "quiet, passive, patient refusal to do the wrong."[82] Jesus models this as he resisted by a "meek, uncomplaining, gentle spirit" in contrast to the "bitter, denunciatory, vindictive spirit of the world."[83] Disciples of Jesus do not resist by "violent or forcible means" but "by removing the cause" of evil itself—the kingdom of Satan.[84] Believers do not seek its destruction by participating in the powers through violent means or its institutions of power, because the spirit of evil and violence permeates the institutions themselves. Christians "cannot uphold what [they] *must* destroy."[85] Rather, "the mission of the church is to destroy them without violence,"[86] and Christians "do not use carnal weapons."[87]

Living amid the powers, disciples of Jesus submit but they do not support, and they resist the powers through embodying the nonviolent, gentle, and meek spirit of Jesus. Lipscomb hoped the church would serve as "an ark of safety, peace and security, in which the family of God may dwell in peace and harmony, even while the world and the kingdoms of the world are engaged in fierce and bloody strife."[88]

Practicing the Kingdom of God in the World

Lipscomb often appealed to Jeremiah 29:7 as an operative principle for practicing the Christian life while living among the nations. Judeans, exiled in Babylon, sought its peace but did not "identify themselves with Babylon."[89] They did not seek its peace for the sake of the "prosperity of their wicked enslavers, nor of the government" but "for their own quiet and peace."[90] They trusted God's overruling care in quiet service while avoiding all "violence and political means to better [their] condition."[91]

When the people of God live peaceably among the nations, the nations benefit. When the church, within its own community and through its influence in society, maintains "a high standard of morality" and creates "a public sentiment for virtue and uprightness," it has a leavening impact on culture.[92] It infuses the world with morality, even to the extent that the civil power "enacts laws that promote morality rather than destroy it," as, for example, in the case of polygamy (though Jesus himself did not seek to change Roman marriage laws). "The laws that promote morality and social well-being," Lipscomb argued, "are the indirect and reflex fruits of religion in the world."[93] In this way, the church is able to "remain in the world and yet keep itself free from the spirit of the world," and the church becomes an "active leaven of morality."[94] This is a high view of the church, and an equally high demand upon the community of faith. Precisely because the church has this leavening mission, it should never devote its energies to political processes but only to the life and vibrancy of the church as a leavening community.

Lipscomb is hopeful for, and thinks there is evidence of, the progressive growth of morality in communities influenced by active and vibrant churches. In some ways, the world has grown better due to successive reformations and the formation of Christian character in communities of faith.[95] This is part of the purpose of the church itself. Jesus established it as a "training school in the devil's kingdom" for the overthrow of the evil one and the equipping of the followers of Jesus in kingdom service.[96] Over "generations," Lipscomb believed, society's "sense of right" is "cultivated" and evil is "more clearly" seen, as the "horizon is enlarged and our vision is clearer."[97]

For Lipscomb, the Temperance movement, which captivated many of his contemporaries, illustrated this. While he opposed the participation of Christians in the political process itself—that is, he did not think one should vote for or against Temperance—he thought the church had a leavening influence on the community as a whole. In Nashville, there were "communities in which Christians have not voted for years," but their neighbors generally voted for prohibition more than "any other neighborhoods" because of the "moral and religious influence" of their "example." In this way, Christians led the fight against the sale of whiskey, but they employed "spiritual weapons" rather than political ones.[98] The church exerted its "proper moral influence" rather than engaging in "political strife."[99] And if the government decided to prohibit "intoxicating liquors," he will "thankfully accept it as an overruling of God."[100]

Carnal weapons, whether voting or disturbances, are violent measures. Voting coerces others into morality, and Lipscomb thought it "wrong for religious people to force their religion, or any part of it, on others."[101] Neither should Christians engage in unlawful activities that damage property or create disturbances that are not only disruptive to order but counterproductive. For example, Lipscomb knew an elder that broke into a saloon and emptied it of its alcohol, and he judged the elder in violation of the spirit of Jesus.[102] In either case, if one uses civil power to coerce one's views, then that "same power" may be used to suppress other enemies, which may lead to the persecution of Christians themselves.[103] If Christians take civil power into their own hands to suppress the drink, they may find themselves burned by that same power.

Disciples of Jesus, Lipscomb believed, had the duty to address "all questions that arise in society—that is, to stand on the side of right and justice, to study the moral questions that arise in the affairs of the world, and warn as to the principles of right and justice." And whoever does so "benefits humanity."[104] Thus, though Lipscomb did not march or vote, he was not silent.

Lipscomb knew the social evils of his day. One example is the capitalist/labor struggle in the late nineteenth and early twentieth centuries.[105] He favored the "working man" over the rich industrialists, and he rooted his opposition to the concentration of wealth in the hands of a few in Israel's own economic practices. Though Israel was a spiritual form of the church rather than a pattern for human governments, Israel's practices do offer some wisdom.

> The Bible furnishes protection against social evils. One of the clouds on our horizon is the tendency to the accumulation of extreme riches in the hands of a few

and the extreme poverty of another element. The Bible, in its arrangements for the release of debts, the return of lands, and the general restitution of Sabbatical years and jubilee years, was a preventive of such evils, and teaches a lesson of wisdom the governments of this world have yet to learn.[106]

Israel's economic structures intended to lift the poor out of poverty and hinder the rich from exploiting the poor in the accumulation of more wealth, so that everyone could sit under their own fig tree and have their own vine.

The election of 1896 involved a strong split between wealthy industrial capitalists (typically Republicans) and poor labor (typically Democrats). Lipscomb did not vote, of course, but he spoke. While remaining aloof from the political strife, he taught "justice and right" and pressed "the lesson that the selfish accumulation of money or the selfish exercise of power, without regard to the rights and needs of others" will lead "to a violent end." Because the "sympathies" of Jesus "were with the poor, the laborer, those in humble situation, not with the rich or exalted," "the dignity and honor of labor must prevail and its rights be vindicated." The wealthy must "deal justly" with labor and "cease to legislate for capital" but "help labor," which is a "Christian" as well as a "wise policy" that would avoid violence. Nevertheless, one way or another, in God's providence, "things will be righted."[107]

According to Lipscomb, then, the church practices the kingdom of God under the sovereignty of God as both a *witness* to justice and as an *embodiment* of that justice. Disciples of Jesus are neither silent nor inactive. They speak and act, but they do so in the spirit of Jesus without coercion, disorder, or violence.

NOTES

[1] Richard T. Hughes, *Reviving the Ancient Faith: The Story of Churches of Christ in America* (Grand Rapids, MI: Eerdmans, 1996; repr., Abilene, TX: Abilene Christian University Press, 2008), 117–19.

[2] "World powers" was adapted from the German scholar E. W. Hengstenberg, whose postmillennial commentary on Revelation focused on the conflict between the kingdom of God and "world powers." This was his way of describing the principalities of the evil one located in nation-states; *The Revelation of St. John: Expounded for Those Who Search the Scriptures*, trans. Patrick Fairbairn (Edinburgh: Clark's Foreign Theological Library, 1851–52). Both Fanning and Lipscomb acknowledged their debt. Fanning, "The Kingdom of God Triumphant over the Kingdoms of the World," *Gospel Advocate* 7, no. 7 (July 1861): 197; Lipscomb, "Bro. Men's Article," *Gospel Advocate* 14, no. 44 (November 7, 1872): 1048.

[3] Fanning, "The Kingdom of God Triumphant over the Kingdoms of the World," 193–98; see also "Wars of Heaven and Earth," *Gospel Advocate* 7, no. 7 (July 1861): 199–205; and "May Not Christians Engage in War against Their Brethren or Others?" *Gospel Advocate* 7, no. 7 (July 1861): 217–19.

[4] Fanning, "Suitable Subjects for Discussion in Religious Periodicals," *Gospel Advocate* 8, no. 33 (August 14, 1866): 519.

[5] Lipscomb, *Civil Government: Its Origin, Mission, and Destiny, and the Christian's Relation to It* (Nashville: McQuiddy Printing Company, 1913).

[6] Lipscomb, *The Religious Sentiment, Its Social and Political Influence* (Nashville: Cameron & Fall, 1855), 34.

[7] Lipscomb, "Correspondence," *Gospel Advocate* 8, no. 34 (August 21, 1866): 538.

[8] Lipscomb, "The Gospel Advocate," *Gospel Advocate* 9, no. 10 (March 7, 1867): 185.

[9] Lipscomb, "Our Positions," *Gospel Advocate* 54, no. 34 (August 8, 1912): 952–54; and "Prohibition," *Gospel Advocate* 29, no. 24 (June 15, 1887): 374.

[10] Lipscomb, "The Gospel Advocate," 185.

[11] Lipscomb, "Our Positions," 952–54.

[12] Lipscomb, "Correction," *Gospel Advocate* 34, no. 29 (July 21, 1892): 453.

[13] Lipscomb, "Correspondence," *Gospel Advocate* 8, no. 39 (September 25, 1866): 622.

[14] Lipscomb, "Correction," 453.

[15] Fanning, "Suitable Subjects for Discussion in Religious Periodicals," *Gospel Advocate* 8, no. 33 (August 14, 1866): 518, 520.

[16] Lipscomb, "I Did Wrong," *Gospel Advocate* 8, no. 11 (March 13, 1866): 170.

[17] Lipscomb, *Civil Government*, 128–32.

[18] Lipscomb, "War and Peace," *Gospel Advocate* 8, no. 41 (October 9, 1866): 651.

[19] Lipscomb, *Civil Government*, 129, 131.

[20] Lipscomb, "Does God Take Part in the Conflicts of the Kingdoms of This World?" *Gospel Advocate* 8, no. 2 (January 9, 1866): 23 (emphasis mine).

[21] Fanning, "Suitable Subjects," 518.

[22] Beginning with "The Church of Christ and World-Powers," *Gospel Advocate* 8, no. 2 (January 9, 1866): 28–30, and ending with "Church of Christ and World-Powers, No. 18," *Gospel Advocate* 8, no. 51 (December 18, 1866): 801–5. Lipscomb wanted to publish a pamphlet in both 1867 and 1871 but did not have sufficient funding. "Correspondence," *Gospel Advocate* 8, no. 32 (August 7, 1866): 509; and "Untitled," *Gospel Advocate* 13, no. 31 (August 10, 1871): 740.

[23] Lipscomb, "Closing Volume," *Gospel Advocate* 8, no. 52 (December 25, 1866): 817.

[24] Lipscomb, "Politics Again," *Gospel Advocate* 18, no. 41 (October 19, 1876): 1008–13.

[25] Lipscomb, "The Church of Christ and World Powers, No. 5," *Gospel Advocate* 8, no. 9 (February 27, 1866): 129.

[26] Fanning, "Shall the Gospel Advocate Take Any Part in State Matters?" *Gospel Advocate* 8, no. 3 (January 18, 1866): 34.

[27] Lipscomb, "The Church of Christ and World-Powers," 28–30.

[28] Lipscomb, "An Explanation," *Gospel Advocate* 8, no. 27 (July 3, 1866): 427.

[29] Lipscomb, "Questions for the Editor," *Gospel Advocate* 10, no. 2 (January 14, 1869): 30.

[30] Lipscomb, "Church of Christ and World-Powers, No. 6," *Gospel Advocate* 8, no. 10 (March 6, 1866): 146.

[31] This is the burden of Lipscomb's book *Civil Government*, which I will summarize in the follow paragraphs.

[32] Lipscomb, "Reply to Bro. Lipscomb's Long Article on Politics and Voting," *Gospel Advocate* 18, no. 32 (August 17, 1876): 799.

[33] Lipscomb, "Politics and Christianity," *Gospel Advocate* 15, no. 15 (April 10, 1873): 345.

[34] Lipscomb, "Whose Are the Kingdoms of This World?" *Gospel Advocate* 16, no. 42 (October 22, 1874): 997–98.

[35] Lipscomb, *Civil Government*, 10.

[36] Lipscomb, "Politics and Voting," *Gospel Advocate* 18, no. 28 (July 13, 1876): 657–58.

[37] Lipscomb, "Masonry," *Gospel Advocate* 10, no. 27 (July 2, 1868): 638.

[38] Lipscomb, "Does God Take Part in the Conflicts," 22.

[39] Lipscomb, "Church of Christ and World-Powers, No. 16," *Gospel Advocate* 8, no. 49 (December 4, 1866): 769.

[40] Lipscomb, "Politics and Christianity," 345.

[41] Lipscomb, "May Christians Vote and Hold Office in Civil Government? No. 2," *Gospel Advocate* 22, no. 45 (November 4, 1880): 710.

[42] Lipscomb, "The Christian's Relation to Civil Government—Continued (Read at Huntsville, MO, July 16th)" *Gospel Advocate* 33, no. 40 (October 7, 1891): 628.

[43] Lipscomb, "World-Powers, No. 6," 147–48.

[44] Lipscomb, "Church of Christ and World-Powers, No. 7," *Gospel Advocate* 8, no. 11 (March 13, 1866): 164.

[45] Lipscomb, "Church of Christ and World-Powers, No. 8," *Gospel Advocate* 8, no. 14 (April 3, 1866): 210.

[46] Lipscomb, "Church of Christ and World-Powers, No. 10," *Gospel Advocate* 8, no. 17 (April 24, 1866), 258–59, 262–63.

[47] Lipscomb, *Civil Government*, 23.

[48] Lipscomb, "Church of Christ and World-Powers, No. 10," 258–59, 262–63.

[49] Lipscomb, "Matt. V: 39, 'Turn the Other Cheek,'" *Gospel Advocate* 22, no. 6 (February 2, 1880): 68.

[50] Lipscomb, "Church of Christ and World-Powers, No. 10," *Gospel Advocate* 8, no. 17 (April 24, 1866): 260.

[51] Lipscomb, "The Christian's Relation to Civil Government," 628.

[52] Lipscomb, "Bro. Sommers on Office Holders," *Gospel Advocate* 32 (August 7, 1889): 503.

[53] Lipscomb, "Can Christians Vote and Hold Office? Rejoinder I," *Gospel Advocate* 23, no. 1 (January 6, 1881): 3.

54 Lipscomb addresses Romans 13 on many occasions. See *Civil Government*, 69–82; as well as "The Higher Powers," *Gospel Advocate* 9, no. 27 (July 4, 1867): 521–25; and "The Powers That Be," *Gospel Advocate* 37, no. 35 (August 29, 1895): 548.

55 Lipscomb, "The History of the Early Christians in Their Relationship to Civil Government," *Gospel Advocate* 9, no. 43 (October 24, 1867): 847–48. Cf. *Civil Government*, 116–25.

56 Lipscomb, *Queries and Answers*, ed. J. W. Shepherd (Cincinnati: F. L. Rowe, 1918), 360.

57 Lipscomb, "A Monstrous Dogma," *Gospel Advocate* 23, no. 47 (November 24, 1881): 741.

58 Lipscomb, "The Higher Powers," *Gospel Advocate* 9, no. 27 (July 4, 1867): 525.

59 Lipscomb, "Church of Christ and World-Powers, No. 17," *Gospel Advocate* 8, no. 50 (December 11, 1866): 787.

60 Lipscomb, "Church of Christ and World-Powers, No. 18," 805.

61 Lipscomb, "The Advocate and Sectionalism," *Gospel Advocate* 8, no. 18 (May 1, 1866): 274.

62 Lipscomb, "Politics and Voting," *Gospel Advocate* 18, no. 28 (July 13, 1876): 657.

63 Lipscomb, "Voting and Holding Office," *Gospel Advocate* 23, no. 27 (July 7, 1881): 421.

64 Lipscomb, "Masonry," *Gospel Advocate* 10, no. 27 (July 2, 1868): 638.

65 Lipscomb, "The Christian's Relation to Civil Government," 676.

66 Lipscomb, "Politics and Voting," *Gospel Advocate* 18, no. 28 (July 13, 1876): 657–58.

67 Lipscomb, *Queries and Answers*, 93.

68 Lipscomb, "Samson Shorn of His Locks," *Gospel Advocate* 36, no. 19 (May 10, 1894): 286.

69 Lipscomb, "Politics and Christianity," *Gospel Advocate* 15, no. 15 (April 10, 1873): 338.

70 Lipscomb, "May Christians Vote and Hold Office in Civil Government? No. 4," *Gospel Advocate* 22, no. 47 (November 18, 1880): 742.

71 Lipscomb, "Can Christians Vote and Hold Office? Rejoinder III," *Gospel Advocate* 23, no. 4 (January 27, 1881): 52.

72 Lipscomb, "Prohibition," 374.

73 Lipscomb, "Politics and Christianity," *Gospel Advocate* 15, no. 15 (April 10, 1873): 339.

74 Lipscomb, "Reply to Bro. I. N. Jones," *Gospel Advocate* 16, no. 34 (August 27, 1874): 795.

75 Lipscomb, *Civil Government*, 142.

76 Lipscomb, "Can Christians Vote?" *Gospel Advocate* 10, no. 41 (October 8, 1868): 974.

77 Lipscomb, "The Review on the Position of the *Gospel Advocate*," *Gospel Advocate* 8, no. 42 (October 16, 1866): 661.

78 Lipscomb, "Politics and Religion," *Gospel Advocate* 50, no. 29 (July 16, 1908): 456.

79 Lipscomb, "The Christian's Relation to Civil Government," 676.

80 Lipscomb, "Vote and Hold Office? Rejoinder I," 3.

81 Lipscomb, "The Church of Christ and World-Powers," 30.

82 Lipscomb, "The Christian's Relation to Civil Government," 676.

83 Lipscomb, "The Advocate and Sectionalism," *Gospel Advocate* 8, no. 18 (May 1, 1866): 274–75.

84 Lipscomb, "World-Powers, No. 17," 785.

85 Lipscomb, "World-Powers, No. 5," 132.

[86] Lipscomb, "Can Christians Vote?" 973.

[87] Lipscomb, "Prohibition," 374.

[88] Lipscomb, "The Review on the Position of the Gospel Advocate," 662.

[89] Lipscomb, *Civil Government*, 80.

[90] Lipscomb, "The Christian's Relation to Civil Government," 676.

[91] Lipscomb, "May Christians Vote and Hold Office in Civil Government? No. 4," *Gospel Advocate* 22, no. 47 (November 18, 1880): 742–43.

[92] Lipscomb, "Law and Order," 36, no. 22 (May 31, 1894): 336.

[93] Lipscomb, "Christians and Civil Powers," *Gospel Advocate* 34, no. 33 (August 8, 1892): 516.

[94] Lipscomb, *Civil Government*, 145.

[95] Lipscomb, "Does the World Grow Better or Worse," *Gospel Advocate* 20, no. 6 (February 7, 1878): 86–87.

[96] Lipscomb, "A Monstrous Dogma," 740.

[97] Lipscomb, *Queries and Answers*, 421–22.

[98] Lipscomb, "Prohibition," 374.

[99] Lipscomb, "Religion Purifying Politics," *Gospel Advocate* 24, no. 36 (September 7, 1882): 566.

[100] Lipscomb, "Religion Purifying Politics," *Gospel Advocate* 24, no. 40 (October 5, 1882): 628.

[101] Lipscomb, "The Last Phase of the Temperance Movement," *Gospel Advocate* 16, no. 20 (May 14, 1874): 458.

[102] Lipscomb, "Christians and the Civil Powers," *Gospel Advocate* 50, no. 36 (September 3, 1908): 569.

[103] Lipscomb, "Some Facts and the Lessons They Teach," *Gospel Advocate* 39, no. 41 (October 12, 1887): 646.

[104] Lipscomb, "Some Thoughts Suggested by the Political Context," *Gospel Advocate* 38, no. 47 (November 12, 1896): 724.

[105] See Robert E. Hooper, *Crying in the Wilderness: The Life and Influence of David Lipscomb* (Nashville: Lipscomb University, 1979; rev. ed., 2011).

[106] R. H. Boll, "The Bible School Reunion," *Gospel Advocate* 48, no. 23 (June 7, 1906): 355. Boll summarized an address Lipscomb gave to the gathering.

[107] Lipscomb, "Some Thoughts," 724.

3

From Slavery to Segregation
A Case Study in Lipscomb's Political Theology

JOHN MARK HICKS

The whole idea of churches along race lines is contrary to the spirit and the precepts of the New Testament, and to refuse fellowship to a child of God because of its race or family is to refuse it to Jesus himself.

—David Lipscomb (1907)

At the spring 2018 Student Scholars Symposium of Lipscomb University, several students, under the sponsorship of Richard C. Goode, read papers on David Lipscomb's relationship to slavery and racism.[1] They utilized primary source material (including wills and census reports, as well as Lipscomb's writings) to understand and assess his perspective on slavery and segregation. Their papers called for telling the whole truth about both Lipscomb's biography and the history of Lipscomb University. Their work and courage are much appreciated, and we are indebted to it. This chapter is an attempt to tell the truth and understand the theology of David Lipscomb in relation to race, slavery, and segregation. The search for understanding should in no way diminish the pain of this past nor its evil, and, at the same time, we must understand and tell the full truth (to the extent that we can) before we can move forward in healthy ways.

Lipscomb's goal for the church and for the full reign of God upon the earth was clear: "[The church's] true mission is to break down all principles, prejudices and institutions that divide and sunder [people], that engage in strife and bitterness, and to bind them in one [family], knowing no distinctions of *race*, section, or nation, but all are in one Christ their head.[2]

In another piece, he wrote:

> The true mission of the Christian religion is to raise [humanity] above all these narrow, selfish, sectionalizing influences—to break down these middle walls of separation and strife erected by human selfishness, human ambition, and human wickedness, and to bind all the dissevered, broken, discordant and belligerent factions and fragments of Adam's fallen and sinning family, irrespective of *race*, language or *color*, into one peaceable, fraternal and harmonious body in Christ.[3]

Lipscomb envisioned the church—present in the world through local congregations of Christ-followers—as the locus of reconciliation, peace, unity, and healing. The church is designed to redeem and transcend the brokenness in the world by incorporating all races and nationalities into one community ruled by God.

Lipscomb on Slavery

In 1860, David Lipscomb owned five slaves and Tolbert Fanning owned fourteen.[4] Neither advocated slavery (especially its extension or perpetuity),[5] and both thought slavery, as practiced in the American South, was a great "evil" as a "human, political institution."[6] "Slavery was a wrong," Lipscomb wrote in 1896.[7]

Indeed, though the specifics are unknown, Lipscomb freed his slaves sometime shortly before or soon after the beginning of the war;[8] and before the war, Fanning noted that he and others "aided in purchasing and setting [slaves] at liberty."[9] Also, in one of his sermons, Fanning publicly rebuked a deacon in the church for dividing an enslaved family by selling the father to another master, for which the deacon won a defamation suit in court.[10]

Lipscomb's attitude toward slavery was formed in the womb of his family. In 1831, Tennessee enacted a law that forbade the emancipation of slaves unless the legal authorities of the county permitted it, the freed slaves were removed from the state, and a bond was paid by the owners that was equivalent to the market value of the slave, as security against potential economic damage to the community.[11] Granville Lipscomb (David's father) and Granville's two brothers came to believe "slavery was not in harmony with the principles of the Christian religion."[12] Consequently, one of Lipscomb's earliest memories was the move from Tennessee to Illinois in 1834, where his mother and three siblings died. They moved because they wanted to free some of the family's slaves—at least those they were "at liberty to free and that were willing to go with them."[13] Because the law prohibited freed slaves remaining in Illinois, the freed slaves were transported to Indiana. His mother, wrote Lipscomb, "was a martyr to her own convictions of right, in the effort to benefit and free her own slaves."[14] In the fall of 1835, his father, with the three remaining motherless children and one of his brothers (Dabney), returned to Tennessee and to the slaves they had previously left behind. "He owned slaves after his return," Lipscomb commented, "but always regarded slavery as an evil to the country and to the people. This feeling was cherished in the family. I very strongly imbibed it."[15]

Lipscomb lived among and worked with slaves, both as a young boy on his father's farm in Tennessee and as a manager on his deceased cousin's plantation in Georgia, where he helped Nathan's widow for one or two years.[16] David's father educated his slaves; shared worship with them in his own home, where Africans sometimes led worship; and accepted the institution "under protest."[17] David's experience with enslaved Africans was, he believed, peaceful—even familial. The year after the war, he described his long association with African people:

> We have been their lifelong associates, have played with them in childhood, toiled side by side with them in manhood, have provided for their wants in common with our own, have regarded them as members of our households, have nursed them in sickness, have followed their relatives, and they ours, to the same burial ground, and have wept around the same grave, have attended together the same meetings, sang the same songs, sat around the same communion table of our common Lord, and looked forward to one common hope of rest in the same blessed Heaven, and shall we suffer ourselves to be alienated from them or them from us for no act of theirs or ours?[18]

When Lipscomb returned to Tennessee from Georgia, he contracted with the Winchester-Alabama Railroad Company to extend tracks to Fayetteville, Tennessee, and Huntsville, Alabama. When Granville died in 1853, David was left with the care of his stepmother and younger siblings, as well as a three-hundred-acre farm with several slaves.[19] As a result, he became a farmer in 1854, and this is how he earned his livelihood for most of his life (he taught school during the war for a brief time).[20] Though the last will and testament of Granville Lipscomb only notes that one slave was left to David specifically, it seems likely that other slaves were involved as well, through various family relationships.[21] In 1860,

David owned five slaves, but we do not know how the numbers increased or whether these were the same slaves that were connected with Granville's farm. These enslaved Africans helped him work his 643-acre farm in Bell's Bend near Nashville, which he purchased in 1857. Lipscomb also noted, "We have made more money farming with freed labor than we ever did with slave."[22]

For Lipscomb, like other evil human political institutions, slavery was tolerated by God for some divine purpose, though the reasons are ultimately only "known" to God's own self.[23] In this sense, slavery was "ordained," similar to "evil human governments." Though Scripture "recognized and regulated" slavery, the practice was a function of human governments, and God used the institution created by human political systems for God's own purposes.[24] In this sense, slavery was both divinely "ordained" and an evil. God did not create slavery any more than God created human governments.[25] Slavery was an evil political institution, but even Jesus did not abolish it within the Roman Empire, though he invested his disciples with the responsibility to love their neighbors, which ultimately should have led to the end of slavery.[26] Southern slaves were ultimately freed through violence rather than through the spirit of Jesus, and God's providence liberated them.

Lipscomb often connected slavery with some kind of divine punishment. Joseph was enslaved in Egypt because of his arrogance, and Judah was enslaved in Babylon (innocent Daniel included) due to their sin. Slavery was not racial but connected to some kind of divine purgation and discipline. When Lipscomb was asked about Noah's curse on Ham, he regarded it as a "prophetic" declaration "of what certain families, by their courses which they will pursue, will bring upon themselves." God knew Ham's descendants would pursue such a course, and, in fact, they "were the first to establish government of their own as a substitute for God's government" (i.e., Nimrod in Genesis 10:8). At the same time, God would also curse the descendants of Abraham when they sinned. The curses, however, only last as long as "the line of conduct is pursued" that brought the curse. Lipscomb, consequently, did not see Ham's curse as an immutable racial one. Rather, God decided to bless rather than discipline, and he freed the slaves.[27]

When Europe introduced slavery on the American continent, it became part of the fabric of both the northern and southern states. Over time, the North abolished slavery, and given enough time, Lipscomb believed, the South would have abolished it as well. The economic differences between North and South, as well as sectional mistrust, contributed to the continuation of slavery.[28] Lipscomb did not think slavery was "right," and doubted whether any "Christian master ever bought or sold a slave without some qualms of conscience."[29] In fact, according to Lipscomb, "slavery was an incubus and hindrance to the Southern people," and he was "at all times willing to surrender all [his] interests in it to see it abolished."[30] He believed it would ultimately be abolished, just as it had in the North, by nonviolent means over time. "If the Southern people had been governed by the divine law in the treatment of their slaves . . . God would have opened the way so plainly that they could not fail to see that they ought to free them." In that scenario, the South would have been "blessed" by God. Because the South sought to extend and strengthen slavery, God determined to accomplish the divine "end by the hand of violence." Thus, according to Lipscomb, God decided "to free the slave," and punish both the northern and southern people for its introduction and practice.[31] While "those owning slaves could have *gradually* relax[ed] its bond and freed the slaves without harm to themselves, and with good to the slave," their "selfish interest led them in the wrong direction, and the slaves were freed by a terrible punishment to the North and the South."[32]

In conversation with northern dialogue partners like Isaac Errett, Lipscomb was keenly aware of his southern sympathies and the influence of his context on thinking and life. Just as "Errett's surroundings have developed his political antipathies and sympathies," this was also true of southern people. In fact, if southerners had "been surrounded and associated through life" like Errett, "we doubt not," Lipscomb wrote, "they would have been as resolute and as earnest" as he was. Sectional differences shape perspective, and consequently, "it is difficult for those of one section to realize the feelings, motives, and surroundings" of another. Lipscomb recognized that one's cultural and social location shapes one's "political stand-point." Given this cultural diversity, Lipscomb called for "forbearance" in the midst of sectional strife, as well as the rejection of any political partisanship that subverts the interests of the Prince of Peace.[33]

Nevertheless, the South, Lipscomb thought, should have recognized the evil and sought ways to end slavery. Even if one employs the curse of Ham as a rationale and believes "a nation, a people, or an individual is cursed by God, it does not necessarily follow that good people can participate in inflicting evils God brings upon them," and they certainly should not delight or "rejoice" in those afflictions.[34] But why, then, did Lipscomb own slaves? Perhaps he had a changed perspective by 1868, or perhaps, though he owned slaves, he did not inflict evil upon them but treated them kindly and compassionately under a political system he could not change and where it was difficult, even prohibitive, to free slaves. We do not know, and Lipscomb never fully explained himself.

Lipscomb, like Alexander Campbell, was a gradualist. Regarding slavery as a political institution recognized and regulated by Scripture, he believed the institution would gradually disappear through nonviolent means as the moral level of the

65

nation rose. Gradualism was not uncommon in the South, including in Tennessee. When the 1834 convention gathered to frame a new constitution for Tennessee, the gradual liberation of slaves was considered at some length, and gradual emancipation was supported by a significant number of representatives, particularly from the eastern counties. One proposal suggested that beginning on a particular date, all persons born to slaves would be regarded as free. However, gradualist measures did not win a place in Tennessee's new constitution.[35]

Why was Lipscomb a gradualist rather than an abolitionist? His rationale was similar to Campbell's. It was a political question rather than a moral one. How slaves are treated is a moral question, but whether any people are enslaved is a political one. Underlying this judgment is his hermeneutical commitment—if Jesus did not abolish slavery as a political institution, then the church was not required to abolish slavery as a political institution. As a regulated human institution permitted by God, Lipscomb trusted God would bring an end to slavery in God's own time while Christians treated their slaves ethically, as Scripture demanded. He hoped that end would come through the moral leavening the church would provide.

Though the South should have abolished slavery because it was an evil political institution, Lipscomb nevertheless believed that the "institution of slavery [had] been no disadvantage to the" enslaved Africans, who in their "native land, [were] ignorant, degraded, brutish." Their forced migration (itself an evil similar to what Joseph's brothers did) educated, civilized, and "Christianized" Africans, and they reached a higher "degree of intelligence and civilization" than they would have in their native Africa. Nevertheless, slavers did not enslave Africans "for the negro's good, but from the selfish desire to enable themselves to live the life of ease and leisure which they coveted." The combination, according to Lipscomb, of

"Yankee avarice" and "Southern indolence" led to "cruelty" and "wickedness," as well as regulations and practices that were "irreconcilable with right."[36]

What was a relative benefit to the Africans, however, was a moral "disadvantage" to American "society at large." The institution of slavery harmed the South as it refused to give up its practice; and once it "had accomplished all for the negro that it could accomplish," God "destroyed" slavery through "the overrulings of Providence." Now the door was open, Lipscomb believed, for a "higher development of Christian civilization, both to the white and black, than could be attained" through the institution of slavery. Lipscomb hoped that both blacks and whites would place themselves "under the guidance of [God's] Spirit" and thus enjoy a renewal of divine blessings, including "order, beauty, and harmony."[37]

Lipscomb on Segregation

When the war ended in 1865, freed Africans found themselves in a precarious situation filled with racism, suspicion, and hostility. Lipscomb, like others (including African American leaders like Booker T. Washington), believed education (both religious and secular) was the most important agenda for "Freedmen." To this end, Lipscomb helped "Elder" Peter T. Lowery, "an approved teacher of the Gospel by the Church of Christ in Nashville," who had freed his family before the war and lost everything in the war, start the Tennessee Manual Labor University for freed Africans in Nashville.[38] Lowery had been mentored by Tolbert Fanning.

Over the years, Lipscomb would initiate several efforts to fund and start schools for African Americans in Tennessee. For example, in 1905, S. W. Womack, Alexander Campbell (African American), and G. P. Bowser requested Lipscomb's help in beginning a school. Lipscomb "was the first to mention" to Womack the establishment of a school like the Nashville Bible School for African Americans; he promised help and secured significant funding for the project, involving A. M. Burton in the school for additional funds. Womack and others founded a school in 1907, which was later moved to Silver Point, Tennessee, in 1910 but was closed in 1920.[39]

Lipscomb, like practically all thinkers in the nineteenth and early twentieth centuries (including W. E. B. Du Bois), was paternalistic and embraced assimilationism. Both are forms of racism, as Ibram X. Kendi has demonstrated.[40] For this reason, Wes Crawford has legitimately concluded that Lipscomb was "a benign racist."[41] Lipscomb is quite explicit: "God cast their lot with us, and imposed upon us the work and obligation of doing what we can to elevate, educate, and Christianize them."[42] "The negro," he wrote, "needs help. He knows not how to take care of himself or his family." Consequently, Lipscomb urged readers to provide "personal friendship, personal kindness, personal encouragement and advice" to "Freedmen" in the spirit of Jesus.[43]

Thus, Lipscomb exhibited a benevolent paternalism. His concern for free people was genuine and authentic. He fully believed that this approach would ultimately, though gradually, change the world if the church became the sort of witness for which God had designed it. But given the systemic issues of racism and segregation, Lipscomb was unable to extract himself from the dynamic forces that saturated and shaped his culture. In this way, as Christopher Evans describes the renowned social activist Walter Rauschenbusch, Lipscomb was "tragically typical" for his era.[44]

How did all of this translate into congregational life? Lipscomb believed the church should be the place where black and white serve and worship together *in contrast to segregated society*. S. W. Womack, an African American preacher in Nashville, remembered that in 1865, under the leadership of white ministers like

Lipscomb, "blacks and whites worshipped together," and when the Lord's Supper was served, "we were all waited on just alike," in the same way that he was served among black congregations in 1915. However, something changed over the next fifty years. Churches became more segregated, and animosity toward African Americans grew.[45]

Reconstruction and the emergence of the Jim Crow South dramatically shaped the story of black and white churches in the South. In 1874, Daniel Watkins, an African American from Nashville, asked Lipscomb to publish his request for the use of "meeting-houses" so that he might teach Christianity to "the more destitute of my people" that "are willing to hear." Unfortunately, to the dismay of Lipscomb, "white brethren in some places refused the use of their houses at times when unoccupied by themselves." "We do not hesitate to say," Lipscomb added, "that such a foolish and unchristian prejudice should be vigorously and eagerly trampled under foot, and all persons who are driven from the church because the house is used by the humblest of God's creatures, in teaching and learning the Christian religion would bless the church by leaving it." Further, "if the houses are too fine for this, they are entirely too fine for Christian purposes."[46]

Later that year, on October 9, a "consultation meeting" of more than thirty ministers and elders was held by disciples in Murfreesboro, Tennessee. Daniel Watkins was present, and he was commended as a preacher and church planter. On the morning of October 12, the "ordination" committee proposed this resolution:

> Resolved, that we recommend to our colored brethren
> who have membership with whites, whenever practica-
> ble to withdraw themselves and form congregations of
> their own, believing that by so doing they will advance
> the cause of Christ among themselves, and when it is

not practicable so to do, that they receive the attention of their various congregations.[47]

David Lipscomb, who was present at the consultation, took exception to the segregationist resolution:

> The resolution in reference to colored brethren forming separate congregations we believe plainly contrary to the teachings of the Scriptures. The Jews and Gentiles had as strong antipathies as the whites and blacks. They were never recommended to form distinct organizations. The course we believe to be hurtful to both races and destructive to the Spirit of Christ.[48]

When, in 1878, David Lipscomb heard about an African American who was refused membership in a white church, he responded:

> We believe it is sinful to have two congregations in the community for persons of separate and distinct races now. The race prejudice would cause trouble in the churches we know. It did this in apostolic days. Not once did the apostles suggest that they should form separate congregations for the different races. But they always admonished them to unity, forbearance, love, and brotherhood in Christ Jesus. We believe it sinful to do otherwise now.[49]

Ten years later, when he got wind that some ministers were refusing to serve African Americans or to worship with them, he pressed the point again: "I had much rather belong to and meet with a church composed of humble and earnest negro worshippers, than to a church, that would refuse to preach to negroes." He was incensed that anyone would think otherwise. "The spirit that forbids or refuses the gospel and any of its helps and privileges to a single child of mortality is of the earth and is not of God. He who finds such a spirit in his heart ought to know at once he is not a child of God." "What presumption, sin, and rebellion!" he added.[50] Interestingly, David Edwin Harrell characterized this attitude as "atypical racial behavior" in "southern society."[51]

While Lipscomb opposed segregated congregations, he also had a paternalistic and assimilationist attitude toward African Americans within integrated communities of faith. He thought their proclivities to "over-much religiousness or superstition" created obstacles to their "knowing the truth," and it was "a misfortune" that "the colored population ever attempted separate religious organizations or separate worshiping assemblies," which he regarded as "unscriptural," despite the "difficulties" that "might have arisen in their worshiping together." Indeed, "the negroes needed the care, the counsel, the oversight, the instruction of their white brethren." Since "in the providence of God they were freed," it was his Christian "ambition and desire to encourage, instruct, and elevate them."[52] Lipscomb—who was beloved by many African Americans in Nashville and in other places—participated in the assimilationist and paternalistic racism of his time. It is little wonder some African Americans sought independent congregations in light of such racist and patronizing ideology.

At the same time, few white men had the respect of African Americans in the South that Lipscomb had. For example, upon Lipscomb's death, Samuel R. Cassius noted in a tribute that Lipscomb "was an outspoken Christian man. With him, all unrighteousness was sin, and all human beings were alike to him. He regarded the negro as a man, and a negro Christian as a brother," though Cassius recognized "he could not meet the negro as a social equal and still maintain a useful place in the ranks of his own race." Despite that, "in his death the colored disciples have lost one of their best friends."[53] The four "colored" churches of Christ in Nashville issued several resolutions in honor of Lipscomb, including this: "Resolved, that we cherish his memory and remember with love and affection his modest, but ever emphatic, loyalty to the work."[54] Yet, despite fifteen tribute articles and many expressions of sympathy, no white author mentioned his special relationship with or work among African Americans.

Despite his paternalistic racism, Lipscomb, nevertheless, had harsh words for the whites who encouraged separate congregations. He suggested northern whites encouraged and promoted this tactic as part of their agenda during Reconstruction, which southerners continued during the Jim Crow era:

> The whites who came into the country to use the blacks for selfish ends, encouraged the forming of separate churches that through these organizations they might control the blacks. The white members of the churches of [the South], when themselves not guilty of a narrow and unworthy prejudice against church association with the colored members, gave way to a cowardly fear of the prejudices of others.[55]

Much to Lipscomb's dismay, even "outrage," whites and blacks "are separate and must remain so as a whole for the present. They must be taught now in separate assemblies or the freedmen go without teaching." But it should not have been so. There were no "separate church organizations or worshipping assemblies for" Jews and Gentiles in the New Testament, and there should be none now. On the contrary, an integrated congregation was an opportunity to demonstrate "the power of the Christian religion to harmonize the discordant races in one church."[56]

By 1915, segregation had few exceptions. Womack noted that "only a few of the whites have much or any confidence in the black man, and so many have none."[57] African Americans now worshiped in congregations segregated by the attitudes formed by the Jim Crow South, though Lipscomb himself in 1907 "had never attended a church that negroes did not attend."[58] There were, of course, segregated churches before the Civil War. The first African American congregation in Nashville was planted in 1859. Segregated congregations increased throughout the lifetime of David Lipscomb and S. W. Womack, much to their disappointment. The influence of Reconstruction and Jim Crow shaped how churches segregated themselves into white and black.

From its beginning in 1891, the Nashville Bible School (later known as Lipscomb University) excluded black students. African Americans were not admitted until 1964. The segregation of educational institutions was a given in Tennessee in the late nineteenth century. For example, Atticus Haygood, who lived in Nashville in the 1870s and founded Paine College for African Americans in Augusta, Georgia, in 1882, believed it was "not best to mix the races in Southern school-rooms. Right or wrong, wise or foolish, this is a fact." All "but lunatics and visionaries recognize facts."[59] Moreover, in Tennessee, it was not only a social reality but a legal proscription. An education statute was passed in 1873 that mandated "white and colored persons shall not be taught in the same school, but in separate schools," and this law was renewed in 1901, with imprisonment as a potential punishment.[60]

Church and Society

Given Lipscomb's vision of community in the church noted at the beginning of this chapter, how did Lipscomb believe this would happen in the segregated South? How did he practice the kingdom of God in his context?

On the one hand, Lipscomb still imagined a future where there was one body of Christ without distinction of race or nationality, and integrated congregations lived in peace and love. Lipscomb was "never satisfied of the righteousness of forming congregations in a community along race lines." Though racial and social questions are "difficult and delicate," there is "no doubt as to religious duties and rights," which entails that "Christians of every different nation, tribe, country, of every social and political position, have *equal privilege and rights* in the service of God." Lipscomb believed, just as among Jews and Gentiles in the early church, whatever troubles arise can be "harmonized within the churches" where the "wall of separation" can fall.[61]

On the other hand, the cultural setting of Jim Crow and the antipathies of the recent war and slavery loomed large. Lipscomb offered little comment on the social dimensions of racial relationships. The pages of the *Gospel Advocate* rarely (almost never) discuss racial injustice as a social question, and only occasionally refer to the frequent lynchings in the South and throughout the country.[62] His social witness was fundamentally ecclesial rather than political or activist. As to social realities, Lipscomb is a gradualist. He believed over time, "the religious spirit and practice" would "*gradually* work out the social duties and relations."[63] In another place, he wrote: "The Christian religion did not break up social or political relations. It laid down the principles of religious duty, and left them to *gradually* conform the social and political relations to the principles of the Lord Jesus Christ."[64]

In the light of this gradualism, Lipscomb made some accommodations to the Jim Crow social world. For example, when he described the African American child E. A. Elam and his wife had consented to raise as their own and who attended the same congregation they did (despite the objections of some), he commended the child by noting that she drinks from the cup after everyone else and "deports herself modestly, and is willing to be served last and not participate in the [Bible] class, which shows she does not thrust herself forward as the social equal of the whites."[65]

Lipscomb, we might say, was a realist in this social context. "A few persons or a small portion of a community cannot control the social rules or relations of a community," and if some chose "to associate on terms of equality with the negroes," they would find themselves ostracized by the larger society. Lipscomb thought one had to make a choice as to which circle one would seek to have the most influence for the kingdom. "When [one] cannot associate with both, with which shall [one] associate?"[66]

This seems inconsistent, however, with his insistence on integrated congregations. Lipscomb distinguished between fraternal relationships within the community of faith and other social or political relationships. "The Bible never proposes to disrupt and change social and political relations suddenly," he wrote. He wanted social change, but he believed social change comes through the moral leavening of society as the church embodies the witness of the gospel. Scripture "plants truths in the heart, changes character and life, and as these are modified, fits for changed social conditions; and these come gradually and almost imperceptibly." "To force them is to destroy them," he added. As Christians live out their witness and "cultivate kindly and Christian relations," he believed *the social conditions will adjust themselves.*"[67]

Consequently, though Lipscomb would never refuse any race admittance to any assembly, when a congregation in Maury County, Tennessee, was enthralled in a debate about the attendance of some African Americans, Lipscomb suggested an accommodation to soothe over feelings. Though whites and blacks are equal and have the same spiritual privileges in the context of the church, he suggested they enter and exit through "separate" doors and occupy separate spaces. Lipscomb was distraught over the situation and regretted that any white Christians would have negative feelings about worshipping with any race. "We should fear to meet our Maker with such a record."[68] Nevertheless, his suggestion embodied the Jim Crow dictum "separate but equal."

At the same time, he felt the moral weight of the white neglect of African Americans. "Our treatment of the negro at best," he wrote, "is that of criminal indifference and neglect" and "cruel neglect" at that.[69] Whites must take responsibility. "The failure," he wrote in 1866, "to discharge our duties to a weak, helpless, ignorant, and now truly oppressed people, turned loose in our midst without protectors or advisers, will surely, my brethren, be ours."[70] The exclusion of African Americans from white congregations simply because of their skin color was something Lipscomb never sanctioned. On this, like Paul's defense of Titus, Lipscomb would not yield "for a moment" because to yield is to "encourage" those who object and therefore "sin."[71]

Lipscomb practiced the kingdom of God with flaws. He expected gradual change in social relations through the witness of the church, though he was accommodative in some circumstances to "separate but equal" within congregational life. His hopes for the church were not realized as segregation increased, and the witness of the gospel floundered in the hands of a racist exclusion of black Christians from shared community with white Christians by the vast majority of Churches of Christ. At the same time, while his practice was flawed, his gospel message was clear: God's goal is to bring all people, irrespective of race, nationality, or color, "into one peaceable, fraternal and harmonious body in Christ."[72]

NOTES

[1] The students involved in the symposium were Khylie Arnold, Kaitlyn Boss, Gabriella Cannone, Kathryn Climaco Benitez, Morgan DeLong, Haley Garrick, Sheri Jones, Jacob Maimstrom, Monserrat Molina, Alyssa Ollis, Emily Ridings, Mary Elizabeth Roberts, and Scott Wilson.

[2] Lipscomb, "Sectionalism," *Gospel Advocate* 8, no. 12 (March 20, 1866): 187 (emphasis mine).

[3] Lipscomb, "The Advocate and Sectionalism," *Gospel Advocate* 8, no. 18 (May 1, 1866): 275 (emphasis mine).

[4] US Bureau of Census, Eighth Census of the United States: 1860, Tennessee, Schedule 2, Slave.

[5] Lipscomb, "Correction," *Gospel Advocate* 34, no. 29 (July 21, 1892): 453: "I was not an advocate of slavery."

[6] Lipscomb, "The Gospel Advocate," *Gospel Advocate* 9, no. 10 (March 7, 1867): 185.

[7] Lipscomb, "Some Thoughts Suggested by the Political Context," *Gospel Advocate* 38, no. 47 (November 12, 1896): 724.

[8] Lipscomb, "Correction," 453. The date is partly based on the Zellner family memory that Lipscomb did not own any slaves when Margaret married him in the summer of 1862.

[9] Fanning, "The Colored People of the South," *Religious Historian* 1, no. 3 (March 1872): 90.

[10] James R. Wilburn, *The Hazard of the Die: Tolbert Fanning and the Restoration Movement* (Malibu: Pepperdine University Press, 1980).

[11] *Private Acts Passed at the Stated Session of the Nineteenth General Assembly of the State of Tennessee 1831* (Nashville: Republican and Gazette Office, 1839), 122. Cf. Charles C. Trabue, "The Voluntary Emancipation of Slaves in Tennessee as Reflected in the State's Legislation and Judicial Decisions," *Tennessee Historical Magazine* 4, no. 1 (March 1918): 56–58.

[12] Lipscomb, "Dr. D[abney]. M. Lipscomb," *Gospel Advocate* 27, no. 22 (June 3, 1885): 339.

[13] Lipscomb, "Correction," 453.

[14] Lipscomb, "Notes of Travel," *Gospel Advocate* 9, no. 30 (July 25, 1867): 584.

[15] Lipscomb, "Correction," 453.

[16] Granville Lipscomb owned thirteen slaves in 1840 and forty-three in 1850; see US Bureau of Census: 1840, Tennessee, Schedule 1, Population; and US Bureau of Census: 1850, Tennessee, Schedule 2, Slave. Nathan Lipscomb owned twenty-four slaves; see US Bureau of Census, Seventh Census of the United States: 1850, Georgia, Schedule 2, Slave.

[17] F. D. Srygley, *Biographies and Sermons* (Nashville: F. D. Srygley, 1898), 153–54.

[18] Lipscomb, "The Negro," *Gospel Advocate* 8, no. 16 (April 17, 1866): 250.

[19] Robert E. Hooper, *Crying in the Wilderness: A Biography of David Lipscomb* (Nashville: David Lipscomb College, 1979; rev. ed. 2011), 45.

[20] Lipscomb, "Destitution, Its Cause," *Gospel Advocate* 17, no. 32 (August 12, 1875): 749.

[21] "Last Will and Testament of Granville Lipscomb," dated September 25, 1853, Tennessee State Library and Archives, Nashville, Tennessee.

[22] Lipscomb, "Destitution, Its Cause," 749.

[23] Lipscomb, "God Uses the Evil as Well as the Good," *Gospel Advocate* 22, no. 40 (September 30, 1880): 634.

[24] Lipscomb, "The Negro," 248.

[25] Lipscomb, "The Advocate and Sectionalism," 274.

[26] Lipscomb, "The Negro," 248.

[27] Lipscomb, "Noah's Curse Upon Ham, &c," *Gospel Advocate* 10, no. 20 (May 14, 1868): 461.

[28] Lipscomb, "Slavery—Where Does the Blame Rest?" *Gospel Advocate* 9, no. 36 (September 5, 1867): 707.

[29] Lipscomb, "Politics," *Gospel Advocate* 18, no. 37 (September 21, 1876): 914.

[30] Lipscomb, "Correction," 453

[31] Lipscomb, "God Uses the Evil as Well as the Good," 634.

[32] Lipscomb, "Some Thoughts Suggested by the Political Context," 724 (emphasis mine).

[33] Lipscomb, "Explanation," *Gospel Advocate* 8, no. 27 (July 3, 1866): 427.

[34] Lipscomb, "Noah's Curse Upon Ham, &c," 461.

[35] *Journal of the Convention of the State of Tennessee Convened for the Purpose of Revising and Amending the Constitution Thereof* (Nashville: Banner & Whig Office, 1834), 87–94, 124.

[36] Lipscomb, "Notes of Travel," 584–85.

[37] Lipscomb, "Notes of Travel," 584–85.

[38] Lipscomb, "Manual Labor School," *Gospel Advocate* 10, no. 11 (March 12, 1868): 255–56.

[39] S. W. Womack, "Among the Colored Folk," *Gospel Advocate* 60, no. 1 (January 3, 1918): 18.

[40] Ibram X. Kendi, *Stamped from the Beginning: The Definitive History of Racist Ideas in America* (New York: Nation Books, 2016).

[41] Theodore Wesley Crawford, "From Segregation to Independence: African Americans in Churches of Christ" (PhD diss., Vanderbilt University, 2008), 48.

[42] Lipscomb, "The Freedmen—Their Condition," *Gospel Advocate* 10, no. 7 (February 13, 1868): 147.

[43] Lipscomb, "The Freedman," *Gospel Advocate* 8, no. 29 (July 17, 1866): 460–61.

[44] Christopher Evans, *The Kingdom Is Always but Coming: A Life of Water Rauschenbusch* (Grand Rapids, MI: Eerdmans, 2004), 255.

[45] S. W. Womack, "Attitude of the Races," *Gospel Advocate* 57, no. 52 (December 30, 1915): 1326.

[46] Lipscomb, "Teaching the Colored People," *Gospel Advocate* 16, no. 12 (March 19, 1874): 281–83.

[47] Unsigned, "Murfreesboro Meeting," *Gospel Advocate* 16, no. 43 (October 29, 1874): 1017–18.

[48] Unsigned, "Murfreesboro Meeting," 1020.

[49] Lipscomb, "Race Prejudice," *Gospel Advocate* 20, no. 8 (February 21, 1878): 120–21.

[50] Lipscomb, "Race Prejudice in Religion," *Gospel Advocate* 30, no. 20 (May 16, 1888): 7.

[51] David Harrell, *The Social Sources of Division in the Disciples of Christ, 1865–1900* (Athens, GA: Publishing Systems, 1973), 398, n. 274.

[52] Lipscomb, "Teaching the Colored People," 281–83.

[53] S. R. Cassius, "A Colored Brother's Tribute," *Gospel Advocate* 59, no. 49 (December 6, 1917): 1189.

[54] "Resolutions from the Colored Churches in Nashville," *Gospel Advocate* 59, no. 49 (December 6, 1917): 1189. The four churches were Jackson Street (including S. W. Womack), Kayne Avenue, Cowan Street, and South Hill.

[55] Lipscomb, "Teaching the Colored People," 282.

[56] Lipscomb, "Teaching the Colored People," 282.

[57] S. W. Womack, "Attitude of the Races," 1326.

[58] Lipscomb, "The Negro in the Worship—A Correspondence," *Gospel Advocate* 49, no. 31 (August 1, 1907): 489.

[59] Atticus Haygood, *Our Brother in Black: His Freedom and His Future* (Nashville: Southern Methodist Publishing House, 1881), 144.

[60] "Black Past: Jim Crow Laws: Tennessee, 1866–1955," accessed February 9, 2019, https://www.blackpast.org/african-american-history/jim-crow-laws-tennessee-1866–1955/.

[61] Lipscomb, "The Negro in the Worship," 489 (emphasis mine).

[62] This is one of a few examples. See David Lipscomb, "General News," *Gospel Advocate* 34, no. 52 (December 29, 1892): 828: "Another stone was toppled from the wall of good order, Dec. 19, by the lynching of a negro at Guthrie, Ky., charged with attempting to assault a woman in that vicinity."

[63] Lipscomb, "The Negro in the Worship," 489 (emphasis mine).

[64] Lipscomb, "The Negro in the Worship," 425 (emphasis mine).

[65] Lipscomb, "The Negro in the Worship," 489.

[66] Lipscomb, "Are the Negroes Neglected?" *Gospel Advocate* 68, no. 24 (June 14, 1906): 377.

[67] Lipscomb, "Are the Negroes Neglected?" 377 (emphasis mine).

[68] Lipscomb, "A Trip to Maury and Hickman Counties," *Gospel Advocate* 20, no. 42 (October 24, 1878): 661.

[69] Lipscomb, "Race Prejudice," 121.

[70] Lipscomb, "The Negro," 250.

[71] Lipscomb, "The Negro in the Worship," 489.

[72] Lipscomb, "The Advocate and Sectionalism," 275.

4

Peaceable Pilgrim or Christian Anarchist
David Lipscomb's Political Theology

RICHARD C. GOODE

To use the human is to reject Divine wisdom and divest ourselves of Divine help.
To use the Divine is to follow Divine wisdom and to seek and rest upon Divine
help. There can be no doubt as to which is the Christian's duty. Then the Christian
most effectually promotes public morality by standing aloof from the corrupting
influences of worldly institutions.

—David Lipscomb (1913)

In his opening paragraph of *Civil Government*, David Lipscomb
posed what, for him, was the central issue of political theology:
"That God's will 'shall be done on earth as it is in heaven.'"[1] These
familiar words from the Lord's Prayer occasion—not only for
Lipscomb, but for all disciples—an enduring challenge. How does
one live in the interval between the kingdom's coming and God's
will being done on earth? Finding himself centuries removed
from the original prayer, what did it mean for Lipscomb to live
faithfully in this "already but not yet" interim? Moreover, what
might his insights mean for our own political theology in the
twenty-first century?

Realist, Transformationist, and Radical Political Theologies

Historically, at least three political theologies have provided guidance for life in the interlude.[2] Given the tension between the "already" (the inauguration of the kingdom some two thousand years ago) and the "not yet" (God's will not yet fully done on earth as it is in heaven), "realists" operate from a political theology that strives to fulfill—as best one can—the demands of both the kingdom *and* the world. In other words, assuming the realities of living in the "already but not yet," disciples must intentionally toggle or effectively pivot between the often competing, even contradictory, ethics of the kingdom and the world. Consequently, the best options occasionally will be the world's fallen ethics and politics, even though one is fully conscious that the choices and tactics are inconsistent with the kingdom.

Some find antecedents for this realist political theology in the fifth century theologian Augustine of Hippo, but the boldest contemporary spokesperson has been Reinhold Niebuhr. Niebuhr affirmed Jesus's vision of a kingdom of love and nonviolence. The Union Theological Seminary ethicist even condemned the theological gymnastics required to reason away Jesus's teachings of love and nonviolence with such artifice as Jesus's driving out the money changers from the temple with a whip. At the end of the day, however, the "ethic of Jesus was not applicable to the task of securing justice in a sinful world," Niebuhr maintained. Or, to state matters otherwise, disciples must honor the realities of the "not yet" and not simply the ideals of the "already." The "already kingdom of God," Niebuhr baldly announced, is neither a historical nor human possibility in a "not yet" world.[3]

"Transformationists," by contrast, find it unfaithful to serve two political masters, swiveling between the ethics of heaven and earth. They too acknowledge the "already but not yet" tension, but their political theology resolves the conflict by the final conversion of the "not yet" into the fullness of the kingdom. Even if God's kingdom might not come in its fullness during the course of human history, disciples are still called to do their part in moving the "not yet" toward its final consummation in the "already."

Like realism, the transformationist political theology also has a long pedigree. In fact, one might find aspects of it in the fourth century's Constantinian shift as Christians acquired the power of Rome to direct (or at least influence) the course of political events.[4] At the dawn of the twentieth century, political Progressives in the United States—contemporaries of David Lipscomb—embodied transformationist political theology by creating a social gospel. The Gilded Age of their late nineteenth century forebears had accommodated the abuses of unfettered capitalism and social Darwinism's "survival of the fittest." Therefore, transformationists like Walter Rauschenbusch, Washington Gladden, Richard T. Ely, and Jane Addams identified the injustices of this urbanizing and industrializing society and brought their political theology to bear on the social evils (e.g., poverty, child labor, abusive business practices). With the power of state legislation at their disposal, disciples could convert the world into what Christians knew it ought to be. Ely announced:

> I take this as my thesis. Christianity is primarily con-
> cerned with this world, and it is the mission of Christianity
> to bring to pass here a kingdom of righteousness and to
> rescue from the evil one and redeem all our social rela-
> tions. . . . The mission of the church is to redeem the world,
> and to make peace with it only on its unconditional sur-
> render to Christ.[5]

Although realists and transformationists differ in their political theology, they do agree on one point. Both believe, as Stanley Hauerwas has noted, that "Christians must make use of politics to achieve justice in the world" because this world's political systems and structures (i.e., civil governments and nation–states) provide the principal path for achieving their visions of justice.[6] Thus, James K. A. Smith—a chastened transformationist—calls for Christians to "get over their allergy to power," embrace the power they have, and operate within the elite "upper echelons of cultural production" to effect the necessary outcomes.[7]

Our third model of political theology, the radicals, is also political, as Richard Hughes notes in Chapter One, yet they forswear the traditional political powers of nation–states and civil governments. Admittedly, the label "radical" can be alarming and problematic. Yet presumptions must not prejudice our reading of history. On the one hand, "radical" refers to the sixteenth century Anabaptist Reformation vis-à-vis the Catholic and Magisterial Reformers of that era. On the other hand, "radical" can also refer to disciples of various eras and traditions who have dug into Christian history to reclaim or restore the "*radix*," root, or original genius of the Christian tradition, which defied first-century social and political conventions.[8] Of these three typologies (i.e., realist, transformationist, and radical), Lipscomb's *Civil Government* clearly advocated a radical political theology.

In general, radicals live by four key tenets. First, the deportment of radicals toward civil governments is generally one of defiance. Consider, for example, Adin Ballou's 1839 address to Boston's Non-Resistance Society in which he questions whether Christians need a sovereign state. Does the state offer something the Christian has not already found in a higher, purer form? Ballou answered his rhetorical questions by announcing that human governments have nothing to provide the Christian. Christians were not only pledged to obey God rather than humans, but every supposedly "good" principle a state might proffer was nothing but an inferior reproduction of what God had already given. Thus, "the will of man (human government) whether in one, a thousand, or many millions, has no intrinsic authority—no moral supremacy—and no right to claim the allegiance of man," Ballou announced. "What then becomes of human government?" he asked. "When it opposes God's government it is nothing; when it agrees with his government it is nothing; and when it discovers a new item of duty—a new application of the general law of God—it is nothing."[9] In fact, some radicals in democratic contexts refuse to vote.[10] This stance on voting, however, is not universal among all radicals.

Second, radicals maintain that "the will to power" is fallen and misguided. Instead, disciples, in imitation of the kenotic Christ (Phil. 2:5–11), divest themselves of such quests for control. The fourth century's Constantinian shift replaced Roman political power with a "Christianized" version. Early Christianity (the "*radix*"), however, did not seek such political power. Instead, it invoked Christ's politics of self-abnegation and the self-sacrifice of power (i.e., the *kenosis* celebrated in Phil. 2:5–11). As Martin Scott maintains, "Sovereignty is not defined through 'good' sovereigns. They can be an example of a good version of a bad model, but *the model is still wrong, it cannot be cleansed. Kenosis* and *agape* are the clear, definitive political ethics of Christ in the 'Already' Kingdom."[11]

Third, in addition to *kenosis*, radicals are committed to agape love for the world. Guided by kenosis and agape, many radicals pursue a life of nonviolence. Fourth, Christ's Sermon on the Mount is the definitive word or standard for determining political theology. As with other political theologies, radicals are hardly uniform. In fact, "Christian anarchists" and "pilgrims" comprise at least two subsets within the radical typology.

Radical Political Theology: Christian Anarchy

Admittedly, the label "Christian anarchy" unsettles. Why partner the loving, affirming ethic of Jesus with a chaotic, destructive ideology like anarchy? Although "Christian anarchy" might elicit strong, negative reactions, it is important to distinguish between connotations and denotations. Popular perception might equate anarchy with violent chaos; yet technically, anarchy has a constructive ideation. Indeed, it describes a profitable historic political theology, with some disciples self-identifying as "Christian anarchists."[12] Central to our purposes here, some historians and theologians have placed David Lipscomb within the "Christian anarchy" fold.[13] However, was David Lipscomb really a Christian anarchist?

For all radicals—both Christian anarchists and pilgrims— questions of power, control, and authority are central. Among nineteenth-century Christian anarchists in particular, historian Lewis Perry has found how "they were striving for, and placing themselves under, the only true and effective government: the government [or kingdom] of God." The problem for these faith-based anarchists, in other words, was "human pretensions to govern."[14] Corinne Jacker concurs, noting how Christian anarchists of every age "derive their philosophical justification from a conviction that the State is a profanation of God's will. To them it expresses man's sinful pride when he tries to take the Lord's place as ethical authority and lawgiver."[15] Only God has the legitimate claim to authority. Thus, as Tripp York describes, "The Christian anarchist is not one who just does not want to be told what to do, as the juvenile anarchist would have it, but is the one willing to embody the kind of freedom that poses an alternative to those in charge."[16] For Christian anarchists, all human-created authorities are weak imitations and counterfeits of God's true and valid authority.

Consider, for example, the life and work of William Lloyd Garrison. Through the Non-Resistance Society's 1838 "Declaration of Sentiments," he gave voice to a radical Christian anarchist political theology, asserting:

We cannot acknowledge allegiance to any human
government; neither can we oppose any such
government by a resort to physical force. We are bound
by the laws of a kingdom which is not of this world; the
subjects of which are forbidden to fight . . . which has
no state lines, no national partitions, no geographical
boundaries, in which there is no distinction of rank, or
division of caste, or inequality of sex. . . . Our country
is the world, our countrymen are all mankind. . . . The
interests, rights, liberties of American citizens are no
more dear to us than those of the whole human race.
Hence, we can allow no appeal to patriotism, to revenge
any national insult or injury. The PRINCE OF PEACE . . .
has left us an example, that we should follow his steps.[17]

Sixteen years later, Garrison took matters further when he engaged
in an inflammatory protest. On July, 4, 1854, Garrison draped a
stage in black. Although the event occurred in Massachusetts, he
placed front and center a large version of the Virginia state seal. He
displayed a small flag of Massachusetts in a subordinate position, off
to the side. The US flag was presented bordered in black and upside
down. As the program began, the itinerary included Henry David
Thoreau reading excerpts from his works, as well as passages from
the Bible. Then, during his keynote address, Garrison burned a copy
of the 1850 Fugitive Slave Law. To further scandalize the audience,
Garrison then burned a copy of the US Constitution, denouncing
it as a "covenant with death and an agreement with Hell." Grinding
the ashes of the Constitution under his heel, Garrison declared,
"Thus should perish all compromises with tyranny."[18]

Consequently, the quest for disciples in this world is not to
discern the better, to create the just, or to establish *the* biblical
civil government. For Christian anarchists, *no* civil government

can wield appropriate authority. As Alexandre Christoyannopolos has explained, "it is precisely this acceptance of God's authority that leads to their [the Christian anarchists'] negation of *all* human authority."[19] Lee Griffith underscores this point when he notes the "widespread misperception of power as a neutral entity." The debate is not over *how* one uses power and authority; the concern is that one *does* use power and authority. "In biblical perspective," Griffith counters, "contrary to the modern myth of power as a possession we wield, power possesses us as if it were a creature or demonic spirit. . . . Power does not restrain chaos. Power is chaos."[20]

In contrast to civil governments, which use force, coercion, and violence as a primary tool,[21] Christian anarchists stress the "already" nonviolent ethics of Jesus as definitive for faithful political practice. Fidelity to those kingdom principles (i.e., loving one's enemy, turning the other cheek, returning good for evil, etc.) means that all forms of force, coercion, and violence are always "off the table." Christian anarchy's antistatism and nonviolence, therefore, go hand in glove as Christian anarchists "explicitly reject the state as a bearer of legitimate authority on grounds that it usurps a role to which God alone has the right," as Craig Hovey has found. "When [civil government] depends on the use of force for ensuring its survival, furthering its economic ambitions, or assuring social conformity, the state discloses its fundamental opposition to the peaceable kingdom that Jesus announced."[22]

To this point, Christian anarchists and pilgrims work from the same radical tenets, yet there is a subtle, albeit important, distinction. As mentioned previously, it is a trademark of radicalism to defy civil governments. Nonetheless, the form of defiance is key. Christian anarchists engage in confrontational forms of protest and dissent. Pilgrims, by contrast, are committed to an intentional quiet witness.

When it comes to Christian anarchy's *prophetic agitation* and *resistance*, Dorothy Day provides a helpful case study. As a young adult, Day embraced socialist philosophy as her political means to contest America's injustices; but in 1928, she began finding her politics in the "already." Thus, with the mentoring of Peter Maurin, Day increasingly developed a Christian anarchist approach—which gave rise to the Catholic Worker movement.[23]

Most know the Catholic Worker as a community committed to the corporal and spiritual works of mercy (e.g., honoring Matthew 25's feeding the hungry and housing the homeless). "If we spend the rest of our lives in slums, as I hope we will who work for and read the *Catholic Worker*," Day envisioned, "we are truly living with the poor, working side by side with the poor, helping the poor." Beyond benevolence, however, Day knew that such affiliation with the poor

> inevitably [means we will] be forced to be on their side, physically speaking. When it comes to activity, we will be pacifists, I hope and pray, *non-violent resisters* of aggression, from whomever it comes, resisters to repression, coercion, from whatever side it comes, and our activity will be the works of mercy. Our arms will be the love of God and our brother.[24]

Day's resistance to the civil government could be blunt and scandalous. For example, despite the government's "God talk" (e.g., phrases such as "In God We Trust" and "One nation under God"), she indicted the US's Cold War realpolitik as fundamentally atheistic. "It has become expedient that we murder," Day wrote. "It has become expedient that we ignore the precepts of Jesus Christ laid down in the Sermon on the Mount. . . . Christianity has been reduced to a rule of expediency." To the extent that such expedience lies at the heart of American political thought, Day concluded, "it is better that the United States be liquidated than that she survive by war."[25]

In expression of her prophetic antagonism, Day chose to protest and agitate. When in 1957 the state of New York required civil defense nuclear attack drills—which required citizens to practice escaping to fallout shelters—she used the opportunity to remain in New York City's Central Park, demonstrating against the government policies. She practiced civil disobedience and sought arrest. She explained that "self-suffering" resistance to the civil governments was

> an alternative offered by the pacifist to the government, setting an example—an example which the government could follow, were it a Christian government, in its relations with other states. If the government followed the same technique of endurance and suffering, and offered no resistance to the threatened bombing by another, it would be the beginning of peace.[26]

Over the course of her life, Day was frequently arrested and served several stints in jail for her acts of civil disobedience.[27]

Such provocative demonstrations have been a Christian anarchist brand. Inspired by Day, for example, Phil and Dan Berrigan and the Catonsville Nine contested US military involvement in Vietnam when, in 1968, they entered a Baltimore-area Selective Service office to steal and destroy draft files.[28] Inflammatory actions in the spirit of Catonsville have continued for some fifty years, with the Plowshares movement continuing to practice the political theology of Christian anarchy. Theirs is an incendiary witness against the state, as they agitate and provoke, inciting the state to use the full force and fury of its illegitimate authority to punish dissent. In so doing, Christian anarchists believe they are exposing the idolatry of state power and its illegitimacy.

By means of protest in the public square, the Christian anarchist intent is first to expose the ethics and politics that are uncritically accepted in society. Then Christian anarchists seek to introduce the "already kingdom" as the better ethic. In so doing, they embody the age-old tradition of the "holy fool." If the realists' origins goes back to Augustine, and transformationists go back to Constantine, faithful anarchists may trace their lineage back to Diogenes and the Greek Cynics.[29] These potential connections can reveal vital elements of radical Christian anarchy's political theology.

Like anarchists of every stripe, Cynics also have a dubious reputation as pessimists, whiners, and misanthropes. But easy scorn misses their political contributions. Abraham Malherbe explained:

> The Cynic, filled with philanthropy, recognized his goal to be to benefit people. His concern for others did not originate in a sense of duty [to a narrow polis], but stemmed from a real sympathy with human suffering and the unnatural bondage in which men find themselves. Having freed himself from evils, he was conscious of having a mission to free others.[30]

Then as now, parodying what is commonsense and conventional is to court reprisal, which is what happened to the Cynics. Ancient society maligned and marginalized them.[31] Irrespective of the costs, their calling was to "deface the currency of custom," along with "the refusal to live according to mere habit and entrenched opinion."[32] Stated differently, Cynic nonconformity was a means of lampooning authority and flouting social convention.

Cynics like Diogenes chose to live against the grain and to invite social derision, but such was the cost of his calling. "He may be ridiculed, yet he does not care what people think of him," Malherbe continued. "The benefits that people will receive from him will not come to them because he had sought them out or tried to please them, but because they had observed the example he presented them in his life." For example, quite literally, Cynics wore their beliefs on their sleeves, choosing to move in and amid society in cheap, even dirty, clothing. Thus, the Cynics' garb "is taken up as a deliberate act to demonstrate that the simplicity of the soul finds expression in deeds" rather than appearances.[33]

Diogenes's critique of fashion even went so far as to dictate which colors were acceptable to wear. Acquired by a labor-intensive process, for example, purple was a status symbol—the color of the elite power brokers of society (e.g., Roman senators and generals). Cynics would have none of it. To see one wearing purple in public screamed "avarice, hubris, arrogance, injustice, profligacy, and so forth."[34] The Cynics preferred, therefore, to appear in public wearing their notoriously cheap and often dirty cloaks as "a deliberate and provocative retirement from any formal public position and duty. Worn deliberately, the cloak speaks eloquently: here is a philosophy of action."[35]

Thus, as a matter of vocation, Cynics strove to be systematically and strategically confrontational. Theirs was a studied "shame-lessness" (*anaideia*). With society allowing so many pretenses to persist unquestioned and unchallenged, someone had to take up the call to confront the failures head on. As the clear-sighted, truly free individual, the Cynic felt duty bound to confront neighbors "with *parresia* [frankness] and to act as an example. He did so because of this *philanthropia*, his desire to do good to all people."[36]

To make their larger point, Cynics refused to participate in "politics" as popularly defined and practiced. For instance, the notion of "citizenship"—allegiance to one's own polis—was simply too narrow and restrictive to fulfill the virtue of philanthropia (love of all humanity). City–states were "but the product of all-too-human ambition and delusion," William Desmond avers. "The path to 'utopia' [for Cynics] is not through idealized politics, but through the renunciation of normal political activities, indeed the renunciation of all conventional sorts of power," and "paradoxically, the renunciation of politics is itself a political act, and, like Socrates, the ostensibly apolitical Cynic can claim to play the highest political role."[37] Thus, the Cynics renounced citizenship, which came with personal costs. "Renunciation of custom is capped by the voluntary renunciation of citizenship, and the acceptance of exile and nomadism as the only way to live," Desmond recounts. This meant that Cynics would experience the loss of civil rights and protections, and this *atimia* (deprivation of rights) meant that they lost access to the "law courts, temples, agora, assembly and public buildings." A Cynic could not

> buy and sell in the marketplace or transact business; he could not vote; he could not defend himself in court, and so could be convicted more easily, and thereafter attacked with impunity; and even worse, he could not sacrifice to the gods, thereby angering them also. All this would make life fairly intolerable, and so a punishment of *atimia* was tantamount to exile.[38]

Cynics were resident aliens, dwelling in a city, but without the rights and privileges conferred to citizens of that city.

Thus, Cynics were contrapolis anarchists.[39] As such, they might renounce the political systems and refuse to participate in sectarian political convention, but they would not abandon their responsibilities. "The antisocial Cynics did not withdraw from society," Malherbe recounts. Rather the Cynics remained in the city "lambasting it with unrelenting intensity" for its own good.[40] So it seems with Christian anarchists in US history.

Radical Political Theology: Pilgrims

Our English word "pilgrim" comes from the Latin root "*peregri-nus*," which denotes one who is a stranger or foreigner.[41] As fellow radicals, pilgrims share with Christian anarchists the stigma of living as social sojourners and political aliens, lacking any standing to direct or redirect society. Moreover, pilgrims concur on the four key radical tenets listed previously, yet pilgrims differ from their fellow Christian anarchist radicals in an important way.

Where the Christian anarchist impacts the public square via scripted protest and symbolic demonstration, the pilgrim foregoes such strategy. Pilgrimage, by contrast, situates one in God's metanarrative, striving for apatheia toward the narratives of the civil governments.[42] Thus, where Christian anarchists choose the spectacle of defiant protest as a principal tool, pilgrims are committed to an intentional quiet witness through communal habits and practices.

Perhaps a comparison will help distinguish between Christian anarchists and pilgrims. In the early 1940s, as Dorothy Day was building the Catholic Worker movement, one of her contemporaries, Clarence Jordan, created the Koinonia community in Sumter County, Georgia. Informed by his agricultural education and rural context, Jordan envisioned an interracial community serving as a "demonstration plot" for those with eyes to see. The plan, for instance, was to exemplify the inclusive "God Movement" (Jordan's term for the kingdom of God) to the Jim Crow South. In fact, inasmuch as both Day and Jordan labored to build theologically informed communities that incarnated racial equality, nonviolence, and the Sermon on the Mount, Day traveled to southwest Georgia in 1957 to support Jordan's often assailed community.

Overall, the ends of Day's and Jordan's communities were in sync. Their means, however, differed. As noted previously, Day and other Christian anarchists used forms of protest and street theater to advocate for the kingdom. Jordan would not. In fact, he resisted the very kinds of civil disobedience and public activism that social movements were employing so successfully in the 1950s and 1960s. Ann Coble describes Jordan's belief that staged and scripted events such as marches, boycotts, and sit-ins were contrived, artificial, and inconsistent with the golden rule.[43]

Jordan's daughter, Jan, recalled how he resisted "instigating controversy." Having attended the organizational meetings for civil rights marches in 1963, Jan longed to "do" more—to engage in nonviolent civil disobedience. So she made her best case to Clarence. Listening patiently, Jordan responded, "You can join the march. That's your decision. But if you get arrested, I won't get you out [of jail]."[44] Certainly, Jordan endorsed the vision of Martin Luther King Jr.; Jordan resisted dramatic acts and strategies designed to incite "conflict." It was one thing if a faithful incarnation of the God Movement stoked the ire of bigots. It was something else to pick a fight with racists. For Jordan, "Kononia's practice of nonviolence was characterized more by love than resistance."[45]

Perhaps Clarence Jordan's witness serves as an example of the kind of apocalyptic political theology found in the book of Revelation. In John's Apocalypse, saints are called to moments of silence and renunciation of the world. "By providing this interval of silence," Ryan Leif Hansen counsels, "John invites his audience into the possibility of non-participation in their culture of idolatry." John's point is that the saints must not feel at home or relevant in the world, and their nonparticipation will open space for God's alternative to the world. In other words, the saints "are to participate (in the judgment and new creation) by not participating (in the Roman cosmological discourse of cult and economy)." Although mute and disengaged, the saint's "silence is only considered an absence from the point of view of the world that is being.

judged and dismantled." Silence, renunciation, withdrawal, and exile from the world, therefore, "are the activities that make space for the new creation."[46]

Although it might appear as if pilgrims are abandoning, deserting, or otherwise shirking their responsibilities, to be a pilgrim is less a withdrawal from neighbors and community, and more a renunciation of facades, fictions, and social conventions. To practice such a discipline requires that pilgrims empty their self-will, self-centeredness, and self-justification, freeing themselves from all that society contrives to divide (e.g., nationality, class, race, gender, and ideology). Once emancipated from self and liberated from society, the purified pilgrim heart can replace that which distracts and divides with love—a universal compassion that comes from communion with God alone.

Both pilgrims and Christian anarchists are radicals, yet quiet witness distinguishes their respective political theologies. First, pilgrims demonstrate a tranquility that stills one's frenetic desire for power, control, and influence. Their actions lift the unrelenting burden to make some relevant, world-changing impact. As part of pilgrim political theology, their quiet witness is the willingness to "be powerless, willing to limit our seeming power so God's real power can become active in us, most especially in what we would like to do for God," Maggie Ross explains. "As the ancient desert wisdom tells us, the work of asceticism we do by our own effort is entirely pagan. . . . it is only when we are willing to acknowledge our powerlessness and thus enable God's power to be active in us, that our service becomes Christian."[47] This is a silence of adoration, which finds its hope in God and not the self, watching for and yielding to God's providence (Ps. 38:13–15; 46:11).[48] This silence is also closely aligned with quiescence. Here in the face of geological cataclysm (Ps. 46:2–3), and political chaos (Ps. 46:6), for example, the charge in Psalm 46 is to "be still and know" that God is sovereign (Ps.

46:10–11). Admittedly contrary to most everything society teaches about an appropriately active and responsible life, quiescence (*quies* in Latin and *hesychia* in Greek) is the discipline of standing still yet resilient in the face of life's social and political storms, even while fully cognizant of the storm's destructive capacity.[49]

Second, tranquil, centered, and quiet witness exhibits a dispassion (*apatheia*) toward principalities and their powers. Recall, for example, the dialog between Jesus and Pilate during the Passion Narrative. Pilate tried to wrangle Jesus into the ongoing power struggles between occupier and occupied (e.g., "Are you a king?"). Jesus's attention, of course, transcended Pilate's partisan contest, so Jesus responded to Pilate's threats with aloof silence. "The toxic, phantasmagoric, pseudo-world [Pilate] cannot bear silence," Maggie Ross notes, "for silence reveals it for the delusion it is. It is this noisy world of deception and arrogance that the humble Christ defeats by self-emptying silence." Later, she notes how the church has too often succumbed to "and become part of the kingdom of noise."[50] This quiet witness, in imitation of the kenotic Christ, is a pilgrim trademark.

David Lipscomb's Pilgrim Political Theology

The political theology Lipscomb developed in *Civil Government* resonates with this historic pilgrim tradition. Through some 150 pages, Lipscomb developed a concentrated argument that might be summarized as follows:

1. All civil governments are in themselves evil and rebellion against God.
2. It was the mission and work of Christ to defeat all rival powers and governments.
3. Christian participation in, or cooperation with, civil governments is fornication, adultery, and harlotry.

Thus disciples must:

1. Separate from the systems and structures of any and all civil governments.
2. Stand aloof from the principalities and powers of civil governments.
3. Tranquilly, quietly, and steadfastly practice the kingdom ethic that the world will not fathom and cannot appreciate.[51]

Given his personal experiences during the Civil War, Lipscomb was hardly naïve. He held no utopian vision of the US government (or any other civil government) making Jesus's Sermon on the Mount the law of the land. Lipscomb knew that the politics of Jesus would always be a minority position without political power. The politics of the kingdom, therefore, make for an inconvenient life where the pilgrim is out of sync and out of place. Wherever one is, it is never home. To be a pilgrim, Anthony O'Mahony explains, is an "intensely political act" of displacement.[52] Having chosen such disruption, pilgrims accept the deprivation that comes with a life as a wandering foreigner. Here, Dee Dyas explains the pilgrim identity as one of "exile,"[53] and refugees know the consequences of political impoverishment. Pilgrims lack the voice and the power to control the world in which they find themselves, sacrificing direction over both their neighbors and even their own lives. As Gordon McConville explains, the history and purpose of pilgrimage has been to "express ultimate loyalty to God," which "relativizes all other claims."[54] Such dislocation, displacement, and deprivation places one at real risk. Thus, the pilgrim must trust in God alone. Again, as Dyas notes, for the pilgrim, security comes not from the "current place of their sojourn but the eternal security of heaven."[55] Thus Lipscomb acknowledges that God's "children are pilgrims and strangers in the earthly kingdoms."[56]

Certainly, Lipscomb was a radical. His own theological gene-
alogy charted in chapter four of *Civil Government* established
his place in that historic lineage. Throughout *Civil Government*,
however, Lipscomb shows himself more a pilgrim than an anarchist. "Christians are to be supporters and partisans of none. They
are to be active opponents of none," he directed. "A Christian can
engage in active rebellion against no government. Neither active
support or participation, nor active opposition."[57] Active agitation
and opposition is, of course, a trademark of Christian anarchy.
Lipscomb advocated a steady, quiet witness.

Pilgrims live in the midst of society, but without a "side" in
what is being contested around them. Instead of allowing the
political context to define them, their thinking, and their actions,
pilgrims live their peculiar, kingdom commitments, which will be
nonsensical, utterly irrelevant, and entirely ineffectual in the world
directed by civil governments. That is as it must be for a pilgrim.
They are more likely to be absurdly dislocated and displaced than
leading activists or earth-shaking militants. For disciples who felt
compelled to *do* something "effective," Lipscomb encouraged that
they "stand aloof."[58] Be in society, but always and only as a small
candle in the midst of overwhelming darkness, trusting that the
darkness cannot overcome the Light.

NOTES

[1] David Lipscomb, *Civil Government: Its Origin, Mission, and Destiny, and the Christian's Relation to It* (Nashville: McQuiddy Printing Company, 1913), iii.

[2] The political theology typologies presented in this chapter are intended as representative, yet not exhaustive. H. Richard Niebuhr's classic *Christ and Culture* (New York: Harper & Row, 1975), for instance, outlined five typologies, and over the last seventy years, scholars have amended his taxonomy in numerous ways. The respective types exhibit considerable diversity and flexibility. Although definitions are inexact, their descriptions can still serve as a helpful representation of the political theology landscape. One disclaimer to keep in mind is that typologies are not exclusive and individuals have wisely and beneficially worked across political theology "lines." Political theologies may distinguish wise and conscientious disciples, while not dividing them.

[3] Reinhold Niebuhr, "Why the Christian Church Is Not Pacifist," in *The Essential Reinhold Niebuhr* (New Haven: Yale University Press, 209), 102–19. For other works on Reinhold Niebuhr and Christian realism, see Robin Lovin, *Reinhold Niebuhr and Christian Realism* (Cambridge, UK: Cambridge University Press, 2009); Charles Brown, *Niebuhr and His Age: Reinhold Niebuhr's Prophetic Role and Legacy* (Philadelphia: Trinity Press International, 1992); Larry Rasmussen, ed., *Reinhold Niebuhr: Theologian of Public Life* (Minneapolis: Fortress Press, 1991), 119–35; Jeremy Sabella, *An American Conscience: The Reinhold Niebuhr Story* (Grand Rapids, MI: Eerdmans, 2017), 59–86; and John Stackhouse Jr., *Making the Best of It: Following Christ in the Real World* (New York: Oxford University Press, 2011), 81–113.

[4] Critical of the transformationist approach, James Davidson Hunter notes that the Constantinian will to power is revealed in such classic transformationist phrases as "redeeming the culture," "advancing the kingdom," "building the kingdom," "transforming the world," and "changing the world," for behind such phrases lies "the orientation toward power that underwrites" the "Constantinian temptation." See James Davidson Hunter, *To Change the World: The Irony, Tragedy, and Possibility of Christianity in the Late Modern World* (New York: Oxford University Press, 2010), 280.

[5] Richard T. Ely, *Social Aspects of Christianity* (London: William Reeves, 1889), 53. See also Walter Rauschenbusch, *Christianizing the Social Order* (New York: Macmillan 1912). For a more recent expression, see Mary Beth Rogers, *Cold Anger: A Story of Faith and Power Politics* (Denton: University of North Texas Press, 1990).

[6] Stanley Hauerwas, "How (Not) to Be a Political Theologian," in *Christianity, Democracy, and the Shadow of Constantine*, ed. George Demacopoulos and Aristotle Papanikolaou (New York: Fordham University Press, 2017), 259.

[7] James K. A. Smith, *Discipleship in the Present Tense: Reflections on Faith and Culture* (Grand Rapids, MI: Calvin College Press, 2013), 69, 71. See also his *Awaiting the King: Reforming Public Theology* (Grand Rapids, MI: Baker 2017).

[8] For more on the radical tradition, see Andrew Bradstock and Christopher Rowland, *Radical Christian Writings: A Reader* (Chichester: John Wiley & Sons, 2008); Robert Inchausti, *Subversive Orthodoxy: Outlaws, Revolutionaries, and Other Christians in Disguise* (Grand Rapids, MI: Brazos Press, 2005); and Tripp York, *Living on Hope While Living in Babylon* (Eugene, OR: Wipf and Stock, 2009).

[9] Adin Ballou, "Non-resistance: A Basis for Christian Anarchism," *Patterns of Anarchy: A Collection of Writings on the Anarchist Tradition*, ed. Leonard I. Krimerman and Lewis Perry (Garden City: Anchor Books, 1966), 141–49.

[10] See Ted Lewis, ed., *Electing Not to Vote: Christian Reflections on Reasons for Not Voting* (Eugene, OR: Cascade Books, 2008).

[11] Martin Scott, "Kenarchy and an Eschatological Hope," in *Discovering Kenarchy*, ed. Roger Haydon Mitchell and Julie Tomlin Arram (Eugene, OR: Wipf and Stock, 2014), 98 (emphasis in the original).

[12] One contemporary example of self-ascribing "Christian anarchists" is the Jesus Radicals (http://www.jesusradicals.com).

[13] One edition combining Lipscomb's *Civil Government* and his *Queries and Answers* has appeared under the title *Christian Anarchy: The Works of David Lipscomb* (Kindle Edition, 2017). As a matter of full disclosure, I too have called David Lipscomb a Christian anarchist. See Richard Goode, "The Calling of Crappy Citizenship: A Plea for Christian Anarchy," *The Other Journal: An Intersection of Theology and Culture* (November 2018). https://theotherjournal.com/2018/11/01/the-calling-of-crappy-citizenship-a-plea-for-christian-anarchy/.

[14] Lewis Perry, "Versions of Anarchism in the Antislavery Movement," *American Quarterly* 20, no. 4 (Winter 1968): 770.

[15] Corrine Jacker, *The Black Flag of Anarchy: Antistatism in the United States* (New York: Charles Scribner's Sons, 1968), 6.

[16] York, *Living on Hope*, 15. See also Nekeisha Alexis-Baker's "Freedom of Voice: Non-Voting and the Political Imagination," in *Electing Not to Vote*, 23, where she contends that "refusing to vote can liberate Christians from the American myth of voting-as-voice, can free us to speak in new ways, and can liberate us from seeing the ballot box as the most effective way to promote God's shalom in the world."

[17] William Lloyd Garrison, "Declaration of Sentiments Adopted by the Peace Convention," Fair Use Repository, accessed July 23, 2019, http://fair-use.org/the-liberator/1838/09/28/declaration-of-sentiments-adopted-by-the-peace-convention.

[18] See William E. Cain, ed., *William Lloyd Garrison and the Fight Against Slavery: Selections from* The Liberator (Boston: Bedford Books of St. Martin's Press, 1995), 35–37.

[19] Alexandre Christoyannopoulos, *Christian Anarchism: A Political Commentary on the Gospel* (Lutton: Andrews UK, 2013), 5 (emphasis mine). See also Christoyannopoulos's website for a bibliography of his research on Christian anarchy: https://sites.google.com/site/christoyannopoulos/publications.

[20] Lee Griffith, "Called to Christian Anarchy?" in *God and Country? Diverse Perspectives on Christianity and Patriotism*, ed. M. Long and T. Wenger Sadd (New York: Palgrave Macmillan, 2016), 177, 179.

[21] As Max Weber noted, one of the self-appointed privileges that makes a civil government authoritative is its monopoly on violence. See Max Weber, *Politics as a Vocation* (Philadelphia: Fortress Press, 1972), 2. Or as Leo Tolstoy maintained, the terms "government" and "violence" are synonymous. See Tolstoy, *Government Is Violence: Essays in Anarchism and Pacifism* (London: Phoenix Press, 1990).

[22] Craig Hovey, "Liberalism and Democracy," in *The Cambridge Companion to Christian Political Theology*, ed. Craig Hovey and Elizabeth Phillips (Cambridge, UK: Cambridge University Press, 2015), 213–14.

[23] For more on the Catholic Worker's Christian anarchism, see Jeff Dietrich, "Biblical Anarchism and the Catholic Worker," *Los Angeles Catholic Worker* (April 2007) 1–2.

[24] Dorothy Day, "Beyond Politics," *Catholic Worker* 16, no. 6 (November 1949), https://www.catholicworker.org/dorothyday/articles/166.html (emphasis mine).

[25] Dorothy Day, "We Are Un-American, We Are Catholics," *Catholic Worker* 14, no. 13 (April 1948), 2.

[26] Dorothy Day, "Clarification," *Catholic Worker* 24, no. 3 (October 1957), 2. Long-time Catholic Worker Tom Cornell explained that as Christian anarchists, "we do not get

involved in politics per se." He elaborated, "What is specifically Christian about the Catholic Worker form of anarchism can be found in Aquinas, who said positive laws that are not in harmony with the natural law are not binding for us." This is a classic justification of faith-informed protest, noncooperation, and civil disobedience. See Wayne Sheridan, "Farmer, Anarchist, Catholic: An Interview with Tom Cornell," *Commonweal* (September 1, 2014), https://www.commonwealmagazine.org/farmer-anarchist-catholic.

[27] Day's first stint in prison came in 1917 for protesting at the White House for women's suffrage. Under Alice Paul's leadership, Day joined the hunger strike that was only broken by force-feeding. Ironically, by the time the United States passed the Nineteenth Amendment, Day was moving toward Christian anarchy and she never cast a ballot in her lifetime.

[28] Shawn Francis Peters, *The Catonsville Nine: A Story of Faith and Resistance in the Vietnam Era* (Oxford: Oxford University Press, 2012).

[29] *The Stanford Encyclopedia of Philosophy* lists the Cynics as examples of anarchism in historic political philosophy. See Andrew Fiala, "Anarchism," *The Stanford Encyclopedia of Philosophy* (Spring 2018 edition), ed. Edward N. Zalta, modified November 3, 2017, https://plato.stanford.edu/archives/spr2018/entries/anarchism.

[30] Abraham Malherbe, *Paul and the Popular Philosophers* (Minneapolis: Fortress Press, 2006), 18.

[31] The term "Cynic" comes from the Greek word for "dog." Thus the epithet was imposed by others, intended to scorn, condemn, and deride the movement.

[32] William Desmond, *Cynics* (New York: Routledge, 2014), 78.

[33] Malherbe, *Paul*, 20, 252.

[34] Desmond, *Cynics*, 80, 98.

[35] F. Gerald Downing, *Cynics and Christian Origins* (Edinburgh: T&T Clark, 1992), 206.

[36] Malherbe, *Paul*, 40.

[37] Desmond, *Cynics*, 207.

[38] Desmond, *Cynics*, 113.

[39] Desmond, *Cynics*, 187.

[40] Malherbe, *Paul*, 132.

[41] Ian Reader, *Pilgrimage: A Very Short Introduction* (Oxford: Oxford University Press, 2015), 20.

[42] *Apatheia* is Greek for a discipline that precedes the birth of Christianity. At first glance, the term might appear to be a cognate for the English term *apathy*, but appearances can be misleading. The Greek term for such apathy would be *anaisthesia*—a kind of negligent insensitivity. *Apatheia* offers a far more positive meaning. As Joseph Nguyen explains, it is the art of keeping the "mind free from disordered bodily senses, disordered emotions, and disordered attachments." Joseph H. Nguyen, *Apatheia in the Christian Tradition: An Ancient Spirituality and Its Contemporary Relevance* (Eugene, OR: Cascade, 2018), x. *Apathes*, such as the Desert Mothers and Fathers, detached from social convention, choosing to become strangers to and exiles from the world.

[43] Ann Louise Coble, *Cotton Patch for the Kingdom: Clarence Jordan's Demonstration Plot at Koinonia Farm* (Scottsdale, PA: Herald Press, 2002), 161.

[44] Kay Weiner, ed., *Koinonia Remembered: The First Fifty Years* (Grand Rapids, MI: Eerdmans, 2004), 77–78.

[45] Coble, *Cotton Patch*, 160.

[46] Ryan Leif Hansen, *Silence and Praise: Rhetorical Cosmology and Political Theology in the Book of Revelation* (Minneapolis: Fortress Press, 2014), 105–6, 158–60.

[47] Maggie Ross, *Writing the Icon of the Heart: In Silence Beholding* (Eugene, OR: Cascade, 2013), 114.

[48] Perhaps the great hymn to silence in Christian writing is found in John Climacus's Step 11, "On Talkativeness and Silence." Silence, he celebrates, "is the mother of prayer, freedom from bondage, custodian of zeal, a guard on our thoughts, a watch on your enemies . . . a companion of stillness, the opponent of dogmatism, a growth of knowledge, a hand to shape contemplation, hidden progress, the secret journey upward. . . . The lover of silence draws close to God." Climacus, *Ladder of Divine Ascent* (Boston: Holy Transfiguration Monastery), 158–59.

[49] *Quies* is the state when "the total being becomes integrated, so that there is no more self-seeking dispersion of the passions in all directions. Everything is coordinated and under the influence of grace." See George Maloney, *Prayer of the Heart: The Contemplative Tradition of the Christian East* (Notre Dame: Ave Maria Press, 2008), 43.

[50] Ross, *Writing the Icon of the Heart*, 39, 93.

[51] In Chapter Two, John Mark Hicks provides a close and thorough reading of Lipscomb's political thought and practice. Therefore, this chapter relies upon John Mark's in-depth research to illustrate and substantiate Lipscomb's political theology.

[52] Anthony O'Mahony, "Louis Massignon, the Seven Sleepers of Ephesus and the Christian-Muslim Pilgrimage at Vieux-Marché, Brittany," in *Explorations in a Christian Theology of Pilgrimage*, ed. Craig G. Bartholomew and Fred Hughes (Burlington, VT: Ashgate, 2004), 130.

[53] Dee Dyas, "Medieval Patterns of Pilgrimage: A Mirror for Today?" in *Explorations in a Christian Theology of Pilgrimage*, 98.

[54] Gordon McConville, "Pilgrimage and 'Place': An Old Testament View," in *Explorations in a Christian Theology of Pilgrimage*, 27.

[55] Dyas, "Medieval Patterns of Pilgrimage," 98. As Thomas Merton noted, pilgrims are by definition defenseless. The very nature of pilgrimage is to be without control, security, and self-interest, which puts one at extreme risk in the world. See Thomas Merton, "From Pilgrimage to Crusade," in *Thomas Merton: Selected Essays*, ed. Patrick F. O'Connell (Maryknoll, MD: Orbis, 2014), 192–93.

[56] Lipscomb, *Civil Government*, 90.

[57] Lipscomb, *Civil Government*, 133.

[58] Lipscomb, *Civil Government*, 145–46.

5

Exchanging the Kingdom of Heaven for the Empire of America
The Loss of the Apocalyptic Worldview in Churches of Christ

JOSHUA WARD JEFFERY

The man who votes to put another in a place or position, is in honor, bound to maintain him in that position, and is responsible for all the actions, courses or results that logically and necessarily flow from the occupancy and maintenance of that position. A man who votes to bring about a war, or that votes for that which logically and necessarily brings about war is responsible for that war and for all the necessary and usual attendants and results of that war.

—David Lipscomb (1913)

The year 1917 marked an important, albeit traumatic, time for the Churches of Christ in America. Just months after President Woodrow Wilson asked Congress for a declaration of war against Germany, David Lipscomb lay on his deathbed. As he did so, some of his most treasured beliefs, which he had defended since America had entered another major war, were coming under attack from within and without.

Just eleven years prior, after years of theological controversies in the wake of the Civil War, Lipscomb had declared to the federal census that the Churches of Christ were a separate entity from the mainline and increasingly modernist Disciples of Christ. At that time, the census reported that Churches of Christ had 159,123 communicants, while the larger Disciples had 923,698.[1] By the time of American entry into the Great War, the fellowship of the Churches of Christ was the *largest* peace church in the country. Provost Marshal General Enoch Crowder, the US Army's chief law enforcement officer and implementer of conscription, wrote of Churches of Christ in his report to Congress, "This body has no published creed, but a leading elder stated that the churches believe in 'nonresistance.'" Crowder reported that in 1917, the Churches of Christ had 317,937 members, with 132,755 males who were subject to conscription. Crowder expected that all draft-age male members would seek conscientious objector (CO) status.[2]

The nonresistance of Lipscomb and the Churches of Christ was not just pacifism, however. Lipscomb taught nonresistance in the *Gospel Advocate* from its reestablishment in the aftermath of the Civil War in 1865 until his death in 1917, as well as at the Nashville Bible School. Lipscomb's brand of pacifism sprung from a theology of Christian nonparticipation in human government, which has a long pedigree traced from John Humphrey Noyes's teachings at the Oneida Colony to that of the storied abolitionist William Lloyd Garrison.[3] The preacher Barton Stone, one of the founders of what would come to be called the Stone-Campbell movement, embraced much of Garrison's beliefs about the nature of human government, including the idea that Christian participation in government was sinful. Christian nonparticipation in government, coupled with pacifism and an "otherworldly" orientation where the Christian lives as if the reign of God is on earth as it is in heaven in the here and now, coalesced into what Richard T. Hughes calls an "apocalyptic worldview."

This constellation of beliefs was one of the chief characteristics that separated the Churches of Christ from the mainline Disciples, as well as from Protestant denominations more generally. However, these characteristics also marked the Churches of Christ, sociologically speaking, as a sect. A major hallmark of sectarian groups is their indifference or open hostility toward social institutions and cultural norms, including government.[4] Membership in sectarian groups, then, helps set members apart from the rest of society by marking them as cultural outsiders.[5]

The Churches of Christ emerged as a separate sect from the Disciples as the United States was reforging its identity from that of a provincial nation focused on internal affairs into an externally facing empire and world power. This reforging happened largely between the Spanish-American War and the First World War. While most leaders in the church opposed the Spanish-American War, the conflict itself lasted only a short time, was very popular, and did not rely upon conscription to fill the ranks of the army, and so the patriotism of the sectarian Churches of Christ was not put to a major test.[6] However, the First World War marked a profound shift from the norm. The war was initially unpopular with most Americans, and the government had to resort to conscription in order to have enough soldiers to field a fighting force. Dissent was met with both physical and legal coercion. The Churches of Christ, as the largest peace church in the nation, opposed the conflict, and federal agents, angry vigilantes, and sometimes even their own brothers and sisters in Christ investigated, arrested, or harassed many preachers and outspoken members.

While many leaders in the church were outspoken critics of the war both before and after the United States entered it, those leaders allowed both internal and external pressures to mute their opposition. Conversely, as my colleagues have established previously, during the American Civil War, Tolbert Fanning and David Lipscomb regularly preached against the war and Christian participation in it, regardless of whether the Union or Confederacy was in power, and regardless of whether they faced danger for opposing the war. Such fortitude was absent among leaders during the First World War.

Stated another way, the main causes of the decline of the apocalyptic worldview in Churches of Christ stemmed from the events of the First World War. These causes included the dissemination of widespread propaganda by the US government in favor of the war and against those who would oppose it; the co-opting of the populace (including church members) to surveil opponents of the war, report violations, and apply social pressure to dissidents; the use of coercion by the government in the form of federal, state, and local law enforcement officers who investigated every tip claiming a violation of the Espionage and Sedition Acts; and, ultimately, the surrender of the moral authority provided by the apocalyptic worldview by thought leaders in Churches of Christ in the face of such opposition. While the apocalyptic worldview outlived both the death of Lipscomb and the war, the damage inflicted by the conflict ultimately proved fatal. The rise of Nazism, the coming of the Second World War, and the beginning of the Cold War ultimately resulted in the near erasure of the apocalyptic worldview from the theology of mainline Churches of Christ. Since the wounds inflicted upon the apocalyptic worldview occurred in the context of the First World War, I will focus my narration and analysis on the events of the conflict on the American home front and their effects on Churches of Christ.

World War I and the Churches of Christ

As is well known among historians, Americans were largely unin-terested in joining Europe's Great War in 1914. Woodrow Wilson famously campaigned on the slogan "He kept us out of war"; but after winning reelection in 1916, he led the nation into war the next year. Wilson brought the nation into the conflict for several reasons, including German resumption of unrestricted subma-rine warfare and the interception of the Zimmerman Telegram by British intelligence, which was a diplomatic note that sought to bring Mexico into the war against the United States in exchange for cash, weapons, and support in retaking lands lost to the United States in the Mexican War. Wilson also sought to bring America into the war, however, because he craved a seat at the peace talks. Wilson sought the creation of an international agency that would prevent future conflicts and knew that Europeans would not heed his wisdom unless America helped to win peace on the battlefield. Based upon these reasons, Wilson brought the nation into the war in April of 1917.[7]

Many Americans, however, including many in Churches of Christ, wanted the United States to stay out of the conflict, and many more had no interest in fighting what many termed a rich man's war and poor man's fight. In fact, as Michael Kazin has demonstrated, the peace coalition in the United States before April 1917 was the largest peace movement in American history up to that time.[8] As I have argued elsewhere, facing heavy opposi-tion to the war and limited government resources, Wilson turned to scientific management techniques, including initiating a dis-course of 100 percent Americanism; the use of propaganda to spread this discourse; and the use of this discourse to encourage Americans to keep their friends, neighbors, and relatives under surveillance. These techniques were used together to create an

American "carceral state" that allowed the government to surveil and discipline its population in such a way as to establish a hegemonic, prowar attitude that enlisted the population in enforcing new norms upon society. Stated another way, the federal government succeeded in policing its population by convincing the population to police itself.[9]

Policing the population was made easier by the passage of several draconian pieces of legislation that resulted in the eclipse of civil liberties during the war. Combined together, the Espionage Act of 1917, the Threats against the President Act, and the Sedition Act of 1918 made writing or uttering any criticism of the nation, American allies, the president, the armed forces, or the war a federal offense. Thousands of people across the country were investigated, harassed, intimidated, indicted, arrested, tried, convicted, and incarcerated in state and federal prisons for simply speaking their minds.

Anyone who dared speak against the war, the government, or the president risked being investigated and arrested. Wilson's attorney general, Thomas Gregory, famously remarked that "it is safe to say that never in its history has this nation been so thoroughly policed as at the present time."[10] Political statements are notoriously hyperbolic. In this instance, however, Gregory was not wrong. By my estimate, at least fifteen thousand people were prosecuted by the government for war-related crimes—more than twenty-six people per day over the course of US involvement in the conflict. This is a staggering figure, especially in light of how little the federal government was involved in law enforcement before 1917. This number does not count several hundred other persons who were arrested and prosecuted under the US Code of Military Justice, as well as state level sedition and criminal syndicalism laws across the country.[11]

Gregory's agents were veritably everywhere, investigating everyone: surveilling correspondence and the press through the mail, monitoring telegraph messages,[12] enlisting citizens and even ministers to spy on neighbors and church members,[13] and soliciting tips from citizen committees that went door to door to sell government war bonds and savings stamps.[14] According to Jeanette Keith, historian of the American South, the Sedition Act and government attempts to enforce it resulted in an

> intensity and breadth of surveillance that heralded the birth of the American surveillance state. The Bureau of Investigation, the Military Intelligence Division, and the American Protective League were not just spying on leftists, feminists, pacifists, and immigrants—the "usual suspects" in the history of state suppression of the American left—they were spying on just about everybody, with the gleeful compliance of everybody's neighbors. For rural southerners, this sudden intrusion of federal police power must have been startling indeed. Curse the president, bad-mouth the Red Cross "ladies," and before you knew it, you had to account for your words to a federal agent. And not in New York or Washington, but in the smallest, dustiest, crossroads towns in the rural South.[15]

Dissenters against the war of all stripes, including those in Churches of Christ, would feel this pressure from the ubiquitousness of federal agents quite acutely.

American citizens did not simply face the coercive power of the federal government, however. Wilson also commissioned the famous Progressive and muckraking journalist George Creel to sell the war through the use of propaganda. The propaganda that Creel's committee created and spread was just as totalizing as the eventual surveillance that they helped enable. Creel, in memoirs that he wrote after the war in order to make sure that the Committee on Public Information did not disappear into obscurity, wrote:

> Many a good and mis-informed citizen, who had
> an unformed but vivid impression that the "Creel
> Committee" was some iniquity of the devil, took with
> his breakfast a daily diet of our material from the
> same journal that had given him this impression, met
> us again at lunch when his children came home with
> what the teacher had given them from material we
> prepared, heard us again through our Four Minute
> Men organization when he went to the "movies,"
> where our films might be part of the program, and
> rose to local prominence by the speeches he drew from
> the pamphlets of that other useful organization, the
> Committee on Public Information. Like the truant boy
> who ran away from the schoolmaster, Hugh Toil, he
> found us, recognized and unrecognized, at every turn of
> the road.[16]

It should be noted that Creel's book was subtitled "The First Telling of the Amazing Story of the Committee on Public Information that Carried the Gospel of Americanism to Every Corner of the Globe." Members of Churches of Christ would be asked to determine which gospel they supported: the gospel of the peaceable kingdom of Jesus or the gospel of Americanism backed by the guns of the US Army. While many would support the gospel of Jesus in their hearts, they allowed the gospel of Americanism to control their mouths and actions.

The federal government targeted members of the church who practiced nonresistance and refused to fight or be silenced about their stance on the conflict. At least thirty church members who were conscripted after filing CO claims were incarcerated in segregated "objector" areas at army camps across the country.[17] Political scientist Mark Elrod has also found that at least fourteen members of the church were sentenced to a penitentiary at Fort Leavenworth, Kansas, for their refusal to fight.[18]

An example of one man who refused to be silenced is J. P. Watson, a preacher in Middle Tennessee, who was investigated by the state and the US Department of Justice's fledgling Bureau of Investigation (the forerunner to the modern-day Federal Bureau of Investigation) for preaching to audiences that "he did not think a man could be a Christian and a soldier. They could carry him to battle but could not make him fight." Watson also raised the hackles of the government by criticizing the Red Cross and the Women's Christian Temperance Union as being "money machines that God knew nothing about."[19] Watson claimed that God knew nothing about these organizations because of his adherence to Lipscomb's apocalyptic worldview, which taught that Christians should not take part in any organization outside the local church, including, of course, the government.

While Provost Marshal Crowder expected male members of the church to seek CO status, special agents of the Bureau of Investigation disagreed. Agent B. C. Baldwin investigated G. H. P. Showalter, editor of *The Firm Foundation*, along with his correspondent W. R. Carten, for urging members to seek CO status if drafted.[20] While the bureau dropped the investigation after Carten enlisted in the army to avoid prosecution and Showalter agreed not to publish any more antiwar articles, Agent Baldwin's inquiry resulted in silencing a leading church journal for the remainder of the war.

The government also silenced other leading church journals for teaching nonresistance in their pages. Robert Henry Boll, editor of the *Word and Work*, a premillennial journal, was investigated after publishing an article that criticized the war and discouraged readers from purchasing war bonds. A copy of the article ended up in the hands of the Justice Department, and Boll was investigated for violation of the Espionage Act. A US marshal reviewed the case and also investigated Boll's status as an "enemy alien" because of his German parentage. Upon review, the marshal decided against interning Boll as an enemy alien. After some internal discussion at the Justice Department, Chief of the Bureau of Investigation A. Bruce Bielaski chose to have an agent contact Boll and threaten him instead of having him arrested, even though Bielaski believed that Boll had violated the Espionage Act. In Bielaski's reading of Boll's article, though Boll had urged Christians not to purchase bonds, the rest of his article had appeared sufficiently patriotic to warrant a stern warning instead of an arrest.[21]

In Nashville, the authors and editors at the *Gospel Advocate*, Lipscomb's own journal, raised the hackles of the government. As the late Michael Casey has noted, the *Gospel Advocate* was investigated in 1918 for violation of the Sedition Act after Price Billingsley, a minister and frequent contributor to the journal, wrote a piece criticizing the government. Billingsley, along with *Gospel Advocate* editor J. C. McQuiddy, was summoned to the US Attorney's Office. Both men were informed that if the *Gospel Advocate* issued any more articles that were critical of the government or the war, they would face arrest. McQuiddy and Billingsley were able to convince the US attorney that the *Gospel Advocate* would comply with the law and were released.[22]

In Oklahoma, the Bureau of Investigation focused not only on journals but also on higher education. In August 1918, an agent was dispatched to Cordell, Oklahoma, to investigate the *Gospel Herald*, a journal published by J. N. Armstrong. Armstrong was a graduate of the Nashville Bible School, where he studied with Lipscomb and

James A. Harding, and where he was heavily steeped in the apocalyptic worldview. Armstrong married Woodson Harding, James A. Harding's daughter, in 1898.[23]

Agent D. D. Lamond was sent to Cordell, Oklahoma, to investigate Armstrong after the bureau received a letter from the Post Office Department, which had declared an issue of Armstrong's journal as nonmailable under the Sedition Act. When Lamond arrived in town, he contacted the Washita County Council of Defense, which advised him that the paper was a publication of Cordell Christian College, and that since the college was closed for the summer, the paper had not been published since May. Lamond decided to close his investigation based upon this information.[24]

The response of the County Defense Council was odd, however, because just several days before Lamond was sent to Cordell to investigate, the council had just finished an investigation into the college. The college had attracted the attention of the council because several members of the student body had sought CO status. Once these students had been inducted, they refused to obey any and all orders. The army subsequently court-martialed the students, and they were sentenced to hard labor at Leavenworth.[25]

The council, upon investigating the college, found that Armstrong and the majority of the faculty had taught the apocalyptic worldview, which included pacifism.[26] Furthermore, they found that the chairman of the board, W. D. Hockaday, had refused to buy war bonds, even though he had a significant income. News of Armstrong's pacifism and Hockaday's refusal to finance the war caught the ear of members of the main congregation in Cordell, and some members who previously had problems with Armstrong worked to shut the school down.[27] Angry citizens also painted Hockaday's store in nearby Granite, Oklahoma, the color yellow, as a symbol of his cowardice.[28]

The defense council, in response to student resistance against conscription and because of Armstrong and the faculty's teachings on nonresistance, issued an unlawful order to Armstrong, insisting that the school stop teaching pacifism. The order also required that the college board "be so reorganized that as will unreservedly conform to all military policies and requirements in the present war."[29] In other words, the council ordered that Armstrong and the rest of the board and faculty who were against Christian participation in warfare be removed. The board refused to accept the council's request, but Armstrong offered to resign from his position. College board members then appealed to the State Defense Council, which appointed State Supreme Court Justice Thomas Owen to hold an investigative hearing on the issue.[30] This hearing had no legal precedent, nor would it be legally binding.

Justice Owen proceeded to Cordell and summoned Armstrong and members of the board. The president of the board, W. D. Hockaday, went to Cordell to testify and was confronted by members of the county council, who ordered him and another college board member to leave town. When they refused, the council members incited a riot and threatened Hockaday with mob violence. Hockaday refused to be intimidated by this unlawful act of the council and was able to testify before Judge Owen.[31] Owen, after taking testimony, determined that Armstrong and the faculty had done nothing wrong. According to L. C. Sears, a Cordell faculty member, due to increasing threats of violence, Owen recommended to Armstrong that the college close, and Armstrong disbanded the school.[32] After the college closed, the county council told the bureau during its subsequent investigation that it had ordered the college closed.[33] Regardless of whether Armstrong and the college board closed the college due to extralegal threats of violence or the college was closed due to the order of the defense council, the ultimate responsibility of the closure laid with the

Washita County Council of Defense. Its members harassed Armstrong and the board through threats of violence until the college closed its doors.

With Cordell—the largest college of the Churches of Christ—closed, coupled with the silencing of the *Christian Herald*, the *Gospel Advocate*, the *Firm Foundation*, and the *Word and Work*, the teaching voice of the Churches of Christ on nonresistance was largely stifled for the duration of the war.

The League of Nations Controversy

Once the war ended, President Wilson received the opportunity that he had originally sought by bringing the nation into the war: a seat at the negotiating table. Wilson secured the creation of a League of Nations, which he and many other Americans believed might finally bring peace to a violent world.

While Wilson succeeded in convincing world leaders of the need for the league, he was less successful at home. Many Americans were in favor of the league, but a sizeable group opposed it because they believed its provisions—especially those requiring the US to intervene in wars—would undermine national sovereignty. A much smaller number of citizens opposed the entire Versailles Treaty because they felt the terms of the treaty—and especially the reparations required of Germany—were illiberal and unjust.

While thought leaders in Churches of Christ largely ignored the question of whether the treaty was just, they did struggle over whether they should support the league for two reasons: their historic rejection of war and also their long-standing belief that Christians should not participate in or encourage government. These two commitments placed the constellation of beliefs making up the apocalyptic worldview into heavy tension. Proponents of the worldview were left to ponder which was more important: seeking peace in the world, which would ensure that true

Christians could securely refuse to engage in violence on behalf of the state, or refusing to participate in any type of government, whether it be local, national, or now international. Thus some in Churches of Christ supported the league on the rationale that they believed it could usher in a lasting peace, while others were skeptical because it would endorse international government.

Historian of religion and foreign relations Markku Ruotsila, in his monograph *The Origins of Christian Anti-Internationalism: Conservative Evangelicals and the League of Nations*,[34] argues that Churches of Christ opposed the League of Nations. Ruotsila maintains, by conflating Disciples and Churches of Christ, that the restorationism of leaders in the movement led them to believe that true peace could only be ushered in by the conversion of the world to the principles of the movement. Ruotsila also points to opposition to the league by Henry "Marse" Watterson, editor of the Louisville *Courier-Journal* and a former member of the US House of Representatives (who filled a partial term of 1876–77). Watterson married into the Disciples and, upon his death in 1921, had his funeral at First Christian Church of Louisville.[35] Watterson was a Democrat, had fought in the Confederate Army under General Forrest, and was a solid conservative. Watterson had believed that Woodrow Wilson was also conservative, but after Progressive reforms under Wilson during his first term, he came to reject everything Wilson stood for, including the league. Ruotsila argues, incorrectly, that Watterson's religious outlook with regard to the league represents the movement well as a whole, including Churches of Christ.

If we take the rhetoric in the journals of the Churches of Christ seriously, including the *Gospel Advocate* and the *Firm Foundation*, we will find a vastly different story from the one told by Ruotsila. Some members supported the league, while others opposed it. Arguments over the League of Nations, especially with regard to arguments over pacifism and Christian participation in government, and justice versus peace, serve to suggest that the events on the home front during World War I greatly impacted the beliefs and practices of Churches of Christ.

The editors of the *Gospel Advocate* noted a national agitation in the United States regarding the league and at first took a cautious approach, copying an article from the Disciples' official journal, the *Christian-Evangelist*, claiming that women should have a role in the league. The *Evangelist* writer jested that "the age-long notion that women are more merciful than men may suffer a reversal." An editor at the *Gospel Advocate*, however, suggested that while "some women are more bitter than some men," it would be "easier" for men and women to communicate their desires to government officials than for them to "practice as they preach."[36] Such a statement indicates a level of discomfort with the league, especially in light of Lipscomb's apocalyptic worldview. Another early article about the league in the *Gospel Advocate* "simply" noted that the City of Atlanta had come out in heavy favor of the league and that the "Southern Congress for the League of Nations" was "epoch-making" in its turnout when compared with the gatherings in other cities and regions of the country. However, S. H. Hall quickly shed this cautiousness in a second article on the same page, claiming that the league was none other than an answer to the prayers mandated by Peter and Paul to pray for rulers and nations. Hall denounced the bloodshed that necessitated the Treaty of Versailles but rejoiced over the possibility of the league, telling his readers that they "should give thanks" for their leaders.[37] Hall's argument is almost jarring, considering the fact that not long before, *Gospel Advocate* editor McQuiddy had been threatened by the US attorney for denouncing the war.

However, McQuiddy, unlike Hall, did not equivocate between the violence of the war and the potential of the league. McQuiddy blasted those who had been more "ready to criticize the government than they have been in encouraging the peace league, or peace among all the nations of the world." McQuiddy told his readers that he was not interested in involving himself with politics, nor did he wish to argue that the league would necessarily be successful in its aims. However, he argued that Christians were "under lasting obligations to work for peace, pray for peace, now and so long as they are permitted to live in the world," so they should build up the league instead of attempt to tear it down. To tear down the league was not just wrong; it was "not Christlike."[38]

Another (unsigned) article surveyed other non-Stone-Campbell religious journals, finding that most supported the league and that many believed resistance to the league came from party politics and a dislike of President Wilson in particular. The article called for putting politics away and supporting the league.[39]

Not all *Gospel Advocate* editors and writers were as wholehearted in their support for the league, however. Lee Jackson, in an article in July 1919, advised *Gospel Advocate* readers that the league could bring good or ill:

> If actuated by the spirit of the Prince of Peace, such a
> league might mean the beginning of a millennium of
> peace; but if, on the other hand, it should be actuated by
> a world-dominating spirit of commercial greed, it would
> mean more extensive and bloodier wars than any of
> the wars of the past, with the rights of the people of the
> weaker countries altogether ignored.

Jackson also reminded his readers of the suspension of civil liberties that the war had wrought in the United States, especially against those in the church who opposed the conflict.[40] E. A. Elam went out of his way to criticize those in the church and in the broader Stone-Campbell movement—especially at the

Christian-Evangelist—who supported the league and who lauded former president Taft for his peace work. Elam asked where the accolades were for the Prince of Peace, criticizing those such as Taft who supported the war and then supported "*some* 'peace movement,'" while Jesus was against all war. The heated argument between editors and writers in the *Gospel Advocate* continued for several months after the Treaty of Versailles was rejected by the Senate in November 1919.

Unlike the *Gospel Advocate*, however, the editors at the *Firm Foundation* had much less to say about the league. The *Firm Foundation* barely took notice of the league, and when it did, it often failed to even mention it by name. In an article appearing in February 1919, the journal argued that the nations would have to be constantly engaged in war or give it up. The author optimistically opined that the nations would indeed give up war for at least fifty to one hundred years.[41] In a letter to the *Firm Foundation* from John Dunn in August of 1919, Dunn described the league but never named it, stating that he believed it would bring peace and allow for the spreading of the kingdom of God over all the earth.[42] However, by November, when American membership in the league would be sunk, an editorial appeared arguing that much of the push for the league was grounded in millennial thinking, with many Christians believing that it would usher in a postmillennial thousand-year golden age of peace. The editors, of course, not only rejected this millennial thinking but rejected the idea that the league could ever work to create peace.[43] With that, the *Firm Foundation* fell silent on the topic.

The treatment of the league by the leading journals of the church illuminates the fact that with the death of Lipscomb and the onset of persecution of those in the church who refused to support the war, adherence to the apocalyptic worldview had wavered. Many leaders in Churches of Christ who, before the war, would have rejected any entanglement of Christians and politics were now writing in favor of an international governmental body that would be empowered to use coercion in order to stop the coercion of other governments. The Committee on Public Information's propaganda, the social pressures and collective surveillance that this propaganda created, and the use of the Espionage and the Sedition Acts to prosecute religious objectors to war had led leaders to rethink their positions or fold to the pressure. This meant that the apocalyptic worldview faced increasing pressures leading up to the Second World War. Once the Japanese attacked Pearl Harbor and brought the United States into the war, contemporary thought leaders in Churches of Christ, such as Foy Wallace Jr., saw little problem in jettisoning the whole of the apocalyptic worldview. After the war, the onset of the Cold War, with American interventions in Korea and Vietnam, meant that the apocalyptic worldview took an even harder beating. By the time of the terrorist attacks in the United States on September 11, 2001, little trace of the apocalyptic worldview in Churches of Christ could be seen, except in the writings of historians and theologians. The apocalyptic worldview had fallen victim to the culture of war and of leaders in Churches of Christ who wished to move from the outside to the inside because of propaganda, persecution, and personal desire.

NOTES

[1] US Department of Commerce and Labor, Bureau of the Census, *Bulletin* 103, *Religious Bodies: 1906* (Washington, DC: 1910).

[2] US Army, Office of the Provost Marshal, *Second Report of the Provost Marshal General to the Secretary of War on the Operation of the Selective Service System to December 20, 1918*, by Enoch Herbert Crowder (Washington, DC: Government Printing Office, 1919), 56–58. According to the government, the Churches of Christ had more members than any other recognized peace church in the US at the time the country entered the war. The "leading elder" in this case was most likely J. N. Armstrong, President of Cordell Christian College and son-in-law to James A. Harding. Armstrong attended a conference with Crowder, along with several other members of Churches of Christ, in Washington. See James G. Findlay, *In RE J. N. Armstrong, Violate Espionage Law*, February 15, 1919, National Archives and Records Administration (NARA) M1085, Old German Files (OGF) #352204, 16.

[3] For a full investigation of the pedigree of "Christian nonresistance" from John Humphrey Noyes to David Lipscomb, see Joshua Ward Jeffery, "From Oneida Community Communism to Tennessee Tradition Pacifism: Tracing the Pedigree of David Lipscomb's *On Civil Government*" (conference paper, Stone-Campbell Journal Conference, Knoxville, Tennessee, April 7, 2017).

[4] For a full sociological discussion of sects and sectarian groups, see Ernst Troeltsch, *The Social Teaching of the Christian Churches*, trans. Olive Wyon (New York: McMillan Company, 1927), 1: 331.

[5] For a discussion of religious outsiders and insiders, see R. Laurence Moore, *Religious Outsiders and the Making of Americans* (New York: Oxford University Press, 1986).

[6] David Lipscomb, "The War and Its Lessons," *Gospel Advocate* 40 (August 11, 1898): 508.

[7] For a full discussion of causes of American entry into the First World War, see Justus D. Doenecke, *Nothing Less than War: A New History of America's Entry into World War I* (Lexington: University Press of Kentucky, 2014). For an interpretation of Wilson's war aims, see Thomas J. Knock, *To End All Wars: Woodrow Wilson and the Quest for a New World Order* (Princeton, NJ: Princeton University Press, 1995).

[8] Michael Kazin, *War against War: The American Fight for Peace, 1914–1918* (New York: Simon & Schuster, 2017), xii.

[9] For my full argument in this regard, see Joshua Ward Jeffery, "Prisoners Present Arms: Sectarian Christians and the American Carceral State during the First World War" (master's thesis, University of Tennessee, 2018), 3, https://trace.tennessee.edu/utk_gradthes/5339/.

[10] United States Department of Justice, Office of the Attorney General, "Annual Report of the Attorney General," by Thomas Watt Gregory (Washington, DC: 1918), 15.

[11] Statistics for wartime prosecutions initiated under other statutes are hard to locate. Recently, the National Archives and Records Administration has posted incarceration information for the Atlanta Federal Penitentiary, which include name, incarceration dates, and offense. Similar information, without offense information, has been made available for Leavenworth (the civilian prison, not the military prison) and McNeal penitentiaries. Without offense information, I am unable to determine at this time what prisoners at Leavenworth and McNeil were incarcerated for. However, if the percentage of wartime incarcerations at these prisons are similar to those in Atlanta (at least 23 percent), then more than 675 men were incarcerated in the three extant federal prisons for violation of wartime laws in 1918 alone. This count does not include those incarcerated in military lockups, or in state or local prisons and jails. By my count, 274 men were incarcerated in Atlanta for the violation of wartime laws in 1918 alone. This

count does not include most wartime liquor prohibitions, nor men who were prosecuted under the US Code of Military Justice and incarcerated in military prisons. With those numbers, these statistics would easily double or even triple. Women who were convicted of federal laws were sent to state prisons during this time. At least thirty states enacted sedition and criminal syndication laws that they used to prosecute dissenters. For examinations of individual cases, see Stephen M. Kohn, *American Political Prisoners: Prosecutions under the Espionage and Sedition Acts* (Westport, CT: Greenwood Press, 1994), 20.

[12] Bill Mills, *The League: The True Story of Average Americans on the Hunt for WWI Spies* (New York: Skyhorse Publishing, 2013), 114.

[13] Jeanette Keith, *Rich Man's War, Poor Man's Fight: Race, Class, and Power in the Rural South during the First World War* (Chapel Hill, NC: University of North Carolina Press, 2004), 199–200.

[14] William H. Thomas, *Unsafe for Democracy: World War I and the US Justice Department's Covert Campaign to Suppress Dissent* (Madison: University of Wisconsin Press, 2008), 40–41.

[15] Keith, *Rich Man's War*, 199–200.

[16] George Creel, *How We Advertised America: The First Telling of the Amazing Story of the Committee on Public Information That Carried the Gospel of Americanism to Every Corner of the Globe* (New York: Harper Brothers, 1920), 109–10.

[17] The Swarthmore CO Database contains a large amount of information about many of the pacifists that were inducted into the military even after claiming exemptions. See Anne M. Yoder, "World War I Conscientious Objection," Swarthmore College Peace Collection, September 13, 2013, http://www.swarthmore.edu/library/peace/conscientiousobjection/WWI.COs.coverpage.htm.

[18] Mark Alan Elrod, "'The Churches of Christ and the 'War Question': The Influence of Church Journals" (PhD diss., Vanderbilt University, 1995), 162.

[19] Blaine Danley, *In RE J. P. Watson, Alleged Preacher, Violation of the Espionage Act,* November 22, 1918, NARA M1085, OGF #32336, 2.

[20] B. C. Baldwin, *In RE W. R. Carten, Publishing Article against Enlistment,* May 4, 1917, NARAM1085, OGF #14515, 1.

[21] E. P. Hobson, *In RE R. H. Boll, Alleged Violation Section 3 and Section 1, Title 12 of the Act of June 15 1917,* May 23, 1918, NARA M1085, OGF #171553, 1–3.

[22] Michael W. Casey "From Religious Outsiders to Insiders: The Rise and Fall of Pacifism in the Churches of Christ," *Journal of Church and State* 44, no. 3 (2002): 462.

[23] Richard T. Hughes, *Reviving the Ancient Faith: The Story of Churches of Christ in America* (Grand Rapids, MI: Eerdmans, 1996; repr., Abilene, TX: Abilene Christian University Press, 2008), 152–53.

[24] D. D. Lamond, *RE: Gospel Herald, Cordell, Oklahoma,* September 7, 1918, NARA M1085, OGF #259981, 1.

[25] Findlay, *RE J. N. Armstrong,* 7.

[26] Findlay, *RE J. N. Armstrong,* 11; John Mark Hicks and Bobby Valentine, *Kingdom Come: Embracing the Spiritual Legacy of David Lipscomb and James Harding* (Abilene, TX: Leafwood Publishers, 2006), 17–30.

[27] Johnny Andrew Collins, "Pacifism in the Churches of Christ: 1866–1945" (DA diss., Middle Tennessee State University, 1984), 154.

[28] James G. Findlay, *In RE Cordell Council of Defense,* August 22, 1918, NARA M1085, OGF# 271712, 7.

[29] Michael W. Casey "The Closing of Cordell Christian College: A Microcosm of American Intolerance during World War I," *Chronicles of Oklahoma* 76, no. 1 (Spring 1998): 29.

[30] Casey, "Closing of Cordell Christian College," 30.

[31] James G. Findlay, *RE: Cordell Council of Defense: Willful Misconduct of Office,* August 22, 1918, NARA M1085, OGF #271712.

[32] Casey, "Closing of Cordell Christian College," 33.

[33] D. D. Lamond, *RE: Gospel Herald, Cordell, Oklahoma,* September 7, 1918, NARA M1085, OGF #259981, 4.

[34] Markku Ruotsila, *The Origins of Christian Anti-Internationalism: Conservative Evangelicals and the League of Nations* (Washington, DC: Georgetown University Press, 2007).

[35] Joseph Frazier Wall, *Henry Watterson: Reconstructed Rebel* (New York: Oxford University Press, 1956), 8; "'Marse Henry' Laid to Final Rest amid World Tributes: Louisville, His Old Home, Scene of Notable Gathering of Hosts of Friends and Admirers—Burial Ceremonies Simple, as Was His Life," *Editor and Publisher* (April 8, 1922): 8.

[36] "Women and the League of Nations," *Gospel Advocate* 61, no. 9 (February 27, 1919): 198.

[37] S. H. Hall, "Georgia and the Far Southern Field: Atlanta Is for the League of Nations," *Gospel Advocate* 61, no. 12 (March 20, 1919): 274; "Georgia and the Far Southern Field: Some Observations," *Gospel Advocate* 61, no. 12 (March 20, 1919): 274.

[38] J. C. McQuiddy, "The Peace League," *Gospel Advocate* 61, no. 13 (March 27, 1919): 293–94.

[39] "The Church Rebuking Peace-League Politics," *Gospel Advocate* 61, no. 16 (April 10, 1919): 340.

[40] Lee Jackson, "The Proposed Peace League," *Gospel Advocate* 61, no. 29 (July 17, 1919): 675.

[41] John T. Hinds, "To War or Not to War," *Firm Foundation* 36, no. 5 (February 1, 1919): 1.

[42] John Dunn, "From Brother John Dunn," *Firm Foundation* 36, no. 31 (August 12, 1919): 3.

[43] A. M. George, "Will the Nations Ever Beat Their Swords into Plow Shares?" *Firm Foundation* 36, no. 47 (November 25, 1919): 3.

6

Practicing the Ways of Christ in a World That Knows Not Christ

LEE C. CAMP

In the study of the Bible, he saw the one purpose of God, as set forth in that book, was to bring man back under his own rule and government so to re-establish his authority and rule on earth, that God's will "shall be done on earth as it is in Heaven."

—David Lipscomb (1913)

As seen in the previous chapters, Lipscomb's political theology was rich and multifaceted. It was provocative enough to get him threatened with a lynching. It was threatening enough to precipitate the ire of federal and local officials.

Yet Lipscomb's vision, by and large, was unfortunately lost by the time of World War II. In the wake of that loss, anecdotal evidence indicates that contemporary Churches of Christ generally pursue one of two paths: First, there are those who "hold onto the old paths." Yet it turns out that these "old paths" are not really the old paths that Lipscomb articulated so provocatively. By comparison, they turn out to be relatively trivial arguments over matters of church polity. Second, there are those who have in fact rejected the so-called old paths. Not wanting to be mainline Protestant liberals, and having lost sight of the alternative provided by Lipscomb, they run toward a vanilla-flavored American evangelicalism. This approach depoliticizes the gospel, simultaneously assuming that the American Right, by and large, best captures the nature of our political witness in the world.

I readily grant that this is a too-broad-brush stereotype, and yet my experience tells me there is (too much) truth in the picture I have painted. I think neither of those two options are nearly so interesting, nor nearly so faithful, as the sort of Christian discipleship to which Lipscomb pointed us. To get at this fascinating adventure of discipleship, I would like to discuss six elements of Lipscomb's political theology that may serve us well in our contemporary context and then examine four additional elements that should be challenged, revised, or otherwise reappropriated.

Elements of Lipscomb's Vision to Facilitate Faithful, Creative Christian Discipleship

I see six elements that we might profitably recover from Lipscomb's political theology for our engagement with modern culture. A foundational element to this theology is (1) the assertion that "the biblical topic is politics." Rather than seeing politics as something separable from the gospel, the gospel promises are only rightly understood when construed as inherently political. As a corollary, then, (2) we must recover a construal of the church as a political body. By trying to make the church "religious" as opposed to "political," we actually fail to understand the true nature of the church. But these first two claims must not be wrongly construed as partisan. Thus, we must, as Lipscomb did, (3) steadfastly insist upon the good news of nonsectarianism. Church understood this way may actually provide a third alternative to "right" or "left." While avoiding partisanship, we must also avoid any sort of triumphalism, as if we have any sort of ideologically pure social strategy, (4) because we live between the times and our social engagement must take both sides of this theological and historical assertion—the "now" and the "not yet"—seriously. This eschatological stance then, in turn, (5) provides us a sort of nonutopian realism of bearing witness to the good news in the world. And finally, (6) all these political claims must be underwritten with gospel nonviolence, which is itself yet another political alternative to the so-called wisdom of this world.

"The Biblical Topic Is Politics"

Richard T. Hughes's chapter points us toward a counterintuitive observation regarding Lipscomb's political theology—namely, that it is deeply and inherently political.

It is unfortunate that Lipscomb's vision has been mischaracterized as apolitical—as unconcerned with the political. (And it is unfortunate that Lipscomb's choice of language too many times contributed to and perpetuated this mischaracterization.[1]) But as Hughes rightly notes, we do much better to see Lipscomb's project as *inescapably political*.

Similarly, Richard C. Goode's chapter helps us in this regard. As he notes, Lipscomb makes clear in the preface to *Civil Government* that his project is concerned with human history and the political unfolding of human history: all the pages of Scripture, he suggests, can be summarized in the one longing that God's will would be done on earth even as it is in heaven. Thus with each major move of the story of God's people, we see the sociopolitical struggles at play: a good creation tarnished and vandalized by violence, and various human players and powers awash in blood and coercion seeking to vaunt themselves into places of power, arrogating to themselves a role only rightfully filled by the true Sovereign of all things.

Consequently, Lipscomb's vision—"radical" as it may seem or be—is not unconcerned with politics, social policy, and human history. As John Mark Hicks spells out so well, Lipscomb advocated nonparticipation in certain aspects of "human government," but this by no means necessitated silence on matters of social policy and politics. Quite to the contrary, it is fascinating how "earthly" and well-informed Lipscomb and other late-nineteenth-century Stone-Campbell leaders were regarding social policy. That the so-called apolitical Lipscomb talks a great deal more about politics than many of our leaders today—many of whom have rejected Lipscomb's apocalypticism—is thick with irony.

Thus the "nots" and "nons" that form key elements of Lipscomb's political theology—the "not voting," "nonviolence," "nonparticipation," "nonpartisan," and "nonsectarian"—are not apolitical. Instead, these practices point to an alternative politic. Whether we follow Lipscomb in all the particulars of his contrariness and resistance, we must not miss the profound political witness of his gospel, the profound political nature of the gospel of Jesus Christ. As seen in the shocking tales narrated by Joshua Ward Jeffery, this alternative politic was in fact seen as a threat to the US federal government, and the powers that be flexed their muscle to stifle that threat.

One of the earliest Christian heresies was what we might call an overspiritualizing of the gospel. Various forms of Christian Gnosticism pointed to a sort of religion that did not concern itself with bodily or historical realities. We might want or need to insist in our day that those who want to separate "religion" and "politics" exhibit a similar sort of contemporary heresy. But Lipscomb understood well that the central claim of the gospel—namely, a resurrected Lord—was the primary political claim upon which our faith would flourish or die. Crucified and yet raised, the political turning point of human history had occurred. It was the task of the church to believe this good news and bear witness to the alternative politic made possible by this immense (and to some unbelievable) power of God's Spirit.

The Good News of the Church as Political

A corollary to the previous section is this: the church must be construed as a political body. In William Stringfellow's words, the church is a people that knows the Bible is about "the politics of the nations, institutions, ideologies, and causes of this world and the politics of the Kingdom of God," and consequently learns how "to understand America biblically—*not* the other way around, *not* to construe the Bible Americanly."[2]

Lipscomb, in doing such, provides us a third alternative between Right and Left. Find yourself disgusted with the blasphemous nationalism of the Right? The natural inclination is to run Left. Find yourself disgusted with the self-righteousness and libertinism of the Left? The natural inclination is to run Right. Similarly, we see in the book of Galatians Paul dealing with those of the circumcision party, whom he sharply critiques. In light of their alleged shortcomings, it would not be unexpected for there to form, in reaction, a noncircumcision party. But Paul responds that neither circumcision nor uncircumcision are anything, but a new creation is everything (Gal. 5:15).

In parallel to this, Lipscomb envisions the church as a community bearing witness to, and embodying, this new creation. Such a stance allows us today to see the manner in which both so-called Right and Left are but different manifestations of an immense power struggle of how to construe America. And when Christians get co-opted into the American struggle, either Right or Left, we can see the manner in which those debates are struggling to construe the Bible Americanly, rather than construing America biblically.

But taking Lipscomb seriously allows us to see that we must cultivate in our midst a reading of the Scriptures that forms us into a people capable of understanding America biblically. This surely allows, and may even require, the church to speak clearly, to speak politically, to speak socially in no uncertain terms. So Barton W. Stone would profess the "exciting cause" of his "abandonment of slavery."[3] Or Joseph Thomas would note that some of the Stoneite Christians "*abhor* the idea of *slavery*, and some of them have almost tho't that they who hold to slavery cannot be a Christian."[4] Or the members of the Cane Ridge Church would file twenty-nine deeds of manumission between 1801 and 1819.[5]

There will be here no separation of "secular" and "spiritual," no false divide between the gospel and the political—and yet this gospel is nonsectarian.

The Good News of Nonsectarianism

To assert that "the biblical topic is politics," and to assert that the church is a political body, requires us to qualify: such assertions are not and must not be co-opted into any partisan or ideological agenda.

It is important to note that when one's paradigm for making sense of political discourse is a continuum with the "American Left" on one end and the "American Right" on the other, then one is poised to misunderstand. Such an outlook may misinterpret Barton Stone, with his discourse regarding slavery, as being a partisan of the Left, or could misinterpret Stone at a later time, speaking of the triumph of the church of God over all human governments, as being a partisan of the Right. A fuller understanding would be able to see that he is neither. It is also worth noting that the insistence that we not remain silent on sociopolitical matters means that we may often be wrongly construed as being partisan,

Lipscomb himself transcends and admixes all manner of elements from a variety of parties and perspectives: advocating for labor against greedy robber barons, he sounds unashamedly leftish. Insisting upon the public significance of the Lordship of Jesus, he sounds unashamedly evangelical. His inclinations with regard to race, especially when set in the light of his day, were positively progressive. His critiques of public education, alongside his personal work as an educator and founder of private schools, might infuriate good-hearted liberals. And his acerbic critiques of human governments are something like where the most-Far-Right and the most-Far-Left meet.

Lipscomb can say all these things—and hold them all together in a coherent political theology—because of, not in spite of, the gospel of Jesus Christ. The gospel of Jesus Christ is, among other things, the restoration of fellowship between God and humankind, and consequently the restoration of fellowship among humankind. All the varied parties and sects that postulate great structures of hostility are eviscerated in Jesus of Nazareth. Consequently, any structure that explicitly alienates—or, worse, employs violence against others—must not be obeyed and must not be given our pledges of allegiance.

In other words, the original unity impulse of the Stone-Campbell tradition was not a mere religious impulse but an all-encompassing call to a unity that transcends all kinds of partisanship.[6] Just as the gospel entails sobriety of living in an individual's life, Lipscomb and Fanning remind us that hankering after coercive political power is more "intoxicating" than "alcohol and opium."[7] The call to unity is a call to sobriety from the intoxication of all social forms of hostility.

Where are those among us who can stand as Lipscomb and his allies did in 1860–62, boldly writing a letter to the president of the Confederacy insisting that they would not fight for him?

Or, once Federal forces had taken control of Nashville, Lipscomb and friends writing to the military governor that they would not fight for him, either? Where is the profound political witness of nonpartisanship, the bold profession of faith made manifest in nonsectarianism? Where are those who, like Lipscomb, understood baptism not to be a mere religious talisman but itself a vow—an alternative pledge of allegiance to the King whose lawgiving in the Sermon on the Mount is the ultimate authority? Where are those who, like Lipscomb, can witness a Confederate killing a Yankee, or a member of the Union Army killing a southerner, and proclaim that such violence is not only a violation against one's neighbor but a violation of baptism itself, a violation of the pledge to rise beyond the sectarian hostilities that bloody the theater of human history?

Those of us in Lipscomb's heritage must learn again to see, and to denounce, the deep sectarianism of nationalisms that led to the bloodiest century in the history of the world—with Christian Frenchmen slaughtering Christian Englishmen, German Christians decimating Jews, and American Christians killing Iraqi Christians. Where are those who can say, as Lipscomb said, "I protested constantly that I had not a single enemy"?[8]

Here we begin to see the bizarre nature of the partisanship of "Left" and "Right" among contemporary Churches of Christ. Lipscomb's vision having been lost (or cast off), Left and Right may have little to do with one another "religiously," each perhaps looking down their noses at one another over matters of church polity, in a triumph of a relatively trivial sectarianism. But given that no widely accepted or coherent political theology has replaced that of Stone, Fanning, and Lipscomb (or, I would add, Alexander Campbell), left and right both typically find themselves ill prepared, having few gospel resources to address structures of race, gender, nationalism, and economy. Having cast off the profound political vision of Lipscomb (because "it is apolitical"), we have little to no good news to offer a still warring, fighting, and bickering world.

The "Not Yet" of the Good News

A vision such as Lipscomb's is too often characterized as utopian or unrealistic. This interpretation reasons that if we want to make a relevant difference in the world, then we must not take things like the Sermon the Mount too seriously; we must relegate the "hard teachings of Jesus" to a particular aspect of our lives, rather than taking these things as an ethic for all disciples of Jesus in all aspects of their lives. Otherwise, so this logic goes, we fail to deal with the realities of the world and marginalize ourselves with regard to the stuff that really matters.

This is clearly a false reading of Lipscomb. It is false because Lipscomb does not fall prey to any naive notion that the kingdom of God has come in all its fullness. He does not fall prey to the naive notion that if we are "nice to others, they will (always) be nice to us." We live "between the times" of the inauguration and consummation of the kingdom of God.

This fact—of living "between the times"—has profound ethical implications, several of which are especially relevant here. We are called to live proleptically, to embody the future coming and consummate reign of God in tangible ways, even now.

Also, we must keep a clear understanding of the distinction between the church and the world. The distinction here should not be made in terms of moralistic self-righteousness (for there are hypocrites both in the church and the world); not in terms of what we might call religion (for those who worship military might, global capitalism, experiential consumerism, or NFL football all have their liturgies[9]); not in terms of those who will "go to heaven" and those who will not (for judgments about such are not ours to make, and as Lipscomb makes clear, "going to heaven" is not, after all, the point of the gospel). Instead, one of the primary distinctions between church and world is our confession of the Lordship of Christ, and then all that follows from our pledging allegiance to this Lordship.

Further, it follows that practicing things like baptism (construed as a sociopolitical practice of pledging allegiance); Eucharist (construed as an economic practice of sharing and fellowship); and loving our enemies, forgiving offenses, releasing debts, and the like (also construed as sociopolitical and economic practices) are not naive or idealistic. Instead, they are practices that bear witness to the inbreaking of the kingdom of God. Practicing such, as Lipscomb knew, may lead to one of several ends: because of the beauty and prevalence and power of God, such practices may effect change and reciprocal practices of grace, kindness, and mercy in those who do not yet know the beauty of our Lord. Or, because the kingdom of God has not yet come in fullness, such practices may result in apathetic indifference in others or, more difficult, may precipitate hostility or persecution. But this did not surprise Lipscomb, precisely because he was not idealistic or utopian. He was deeply realistic about the continuing and pervasive nature of rebellion against the gracious ways of God.

The Nonutopian Realism of Bearing Witness to the Good News in the World

That Lipscomb accepts the forthright claims of the Apostle Paul—that the state has a "God-ordained role"—does not, because of all the other elements of his political theology, then fall prey to any sort of naive messianic visions of America. One can, in fact, read Romans 13 (along with Revelation 13) as a realistic nod to the fact that the kingdom of God has not come in fullness, and because of this, governmental powers at their best facilitate a relative peace and at their worst fall prey to demonic delusions of imperial grandeur.

Here, we find a space in which Lipscomb, with all his unwavering insistence upon the way of Christ, facilitates a sort of political realism that may be profoundly helpful. The political realists are helpful in providing a mechanism of checking the pretense of power. Reinhold Niebuhr, for example, was brilliant in his capacity to exhibit the self-interest and self-aggrandizement that works in all the nooks and crannies of institutions of all stripes: any sort of self-righteous messianic pretension only deepens the danger of the self-aggrandizement in providing a false justification.

One could do no better in Hollywood script writing of a tragedy than to have Lipscomb on his death bed with the rise of the specter of the "Great War," in which the religious and scholarly President Woodrow Wilson appropriates Christian language and constructs, casts America as the messiah of the nations, and wages a "war to end all wars." Yet more, as Joshua Ward Jeffery depicts in such horrifying detail, this self-proclaimed Christian president enacts federal policies to arrest, prosecute, and imprison any who would critique the messianic warring pretensions of America. The masters of propaganda in service to such an agenda, who enroll the populace to surveil their neighbors, recount their manipulative deeds under the title "The First Telling of the Amazing Story of the Committee on Public Information that Carried the Gospel of Americanism to Every Corner of the Globe."[10]

In addition to the power of such realism to critique messianic pretenses, such realism also allows us to offer social policy suggestions regarding matters of relative political goods, which I will address briefly as follows.

The Good News of Nonviolence

Lipscomb's vision provides a coherent call to biblical nonviolence as central to Christian discipleship. That calls for nonviolence are often connoted as liberal exhibits again a sharp and unfortunate irony. A refusal to kill one's enemies is conservative with regard to the Stone-Campbell tradition, the great Christian tradition, and biblical authority. The nonviolence advocated by the early forebears in our tradition—Barton Stone, Alexander Campbell, Tolbert Fanning, James A. Harding, David Lipscomb, and many others—stands as a sharp critique to the easy and unthinking acceptance of the warring of the world and the warring of our own nation, which now finds itself in a state of perpetual war.

Even if one cannot go all the way with Lipscomb to his advocacy regarding nonviolence, his witness should draw our attention to the disturbing nationalism and unthinking flag-waving that too often characterizes the (failed) American Christian witness as the military marches off to yet another war. Lipscomb, as well as his teacher Tolbert Fanning, would likely be unsurprised by the fetishes for military might that have characterized the American experiment in the last century.

Four Elements of Lipscomb's Vision to Challenge, Revise, or Reappropriate

There are at least four areas where I want to challenge, revise, or reappropriate Lipscomb's political theology: (1) Lipscomb's false notion of moral culpability that appears to underwrite his prohibition of voting; (2) Lipscomb's sometimes faulty hermeneutical approach to the biblical text as well as some of the problems that arise from this hermeneutic approach; (3) the necessary failure of withdrawal as a sociopolitical strategy; and (4) the ways contemporary scholarship on the principalities and powers can deepen and enrich our understanding of Lipscomb's vision,

Moral Culpability

Consider again this passage: "The man who votes to put another in a place or position, is in honor, bound to maintain him in that position, and is responsible for all the actions, courses or results that logically and necessarily flow from the occupancy and maintenance of that position."[11] This is true only if we allow Lipscomb to define the moral meaning of voting. It is not at all clear that voting entails such an all-encompassing moral culpability. A parent is not "responsible for all the actions, courses, or results that logically and necessarily flow" from bringing children into the world. A board of directors are not "responsible for all the actions, courses, or results that logically and necessarily flow" from selecting any given CEO. The Creator is not "responsible for all the actions, courses, or results that logically and necessarily flow" from creating humankind. It seems dubious to assert that the act of voting carries the sort of moral culpability that Lipscomb asserts.

On the other hand, it is also not at all clear that there is any sort of moral obligation for a Christian to vote. Lipscomb helps us reconstrue the nature and extent of our political activity: the political witness of the Christian church becomes much broader than the mere act of voting. Moreover, given the complexities of coercion that Lipscomb narrates, it does seem that the act of voting becomes morally ambiguous and that we Christians would do better to approach voting with a well-considered ambivalence.[12]

Perhaps a more helpful construct or analog through which to understand voting is that of bearing witness: In what ways might voting bear witness to gospel counsels, which stand In tension with partisanship itself? How might our voting—discerned not in an individualistic act of piety before the "altar" of the voting booth but in shared discernment with fellow believers—bear witness to the alternative politic of the gospel?

Scriptural Hermeneutic

Much has been written on the hermeneutical debates in Churches of Christ, detailing the insufficiency of "flat" or "constitutional-like" readings of Scripture and the insufficiency of "command, example, and necessary inference."

Some examples of such insufficiency are exhibited in Lipscomb's theology. These insufficiencies provide a helpful case study to demonstrate how a more "narratival" reading might be more fruitful. (Recall that a narrative approach often places a priority on construing moral formation and moral action through the cipher of virtue theory.) In what ways might such a focus on narrative and virtue assist us in reappropriating Lipscomb for our own day?

Consider first the notion of silence as prohibitive.[13] Much debate in the Stone-Campbell heritage has occurred regarding whether the silence of Scripture on any given topic is *prohibitive* or *liberating*. That is, if Scripture does not forthrightly *permit* something, then some presume that silence is *prohibitive*, while others assume that the silence *liberates* disciples to do as they wish. So instrumental music in the assembly of the church is not explicitly permitted, for example. Lipscomb and others who saw the silence of Scripture as prohibitive became the strong advocates of a cappella traditions. Those who rejected the notion that the silence of Scripture is prohibitive often became practitioners of instrumental music in worship.

Another approach is simply to take a cue from various virtue traditions, in which the primary task of the church is to embody, enact, or improvise in and out of the biblical narrative. Well-schooled in the biblical narrative, we become adept at enacting the primary thrust(s) and trajectory(ies) of the gospel. Thus, the silence of Scripture on a given matter may, in fact, be pointing to the prudential (but not legalistic or principled) commitment to our own silence or prohibition on a matter. Yet on the other hand, in a different context, such silence in Scripture may open up a liberty for us: prudence, justice, courage, and all the other virtues of the gospel and the fruit of the Spirit must function in such a way that are consistent with the gospel narrative out of which we live.

Consequently, we would not have to choose, say, between the "radical anarchist" or the "radical pilgrim" model. We can celebrate the "anarchist" or "street theater" tactics of Dorothy Day and Shane Claiborne, and we can celebrate the "pilgrim" and "dispassionate" approach of Lipscomb and Clarence Jordan. That is, we can celebrate each in their own turn, given their context, given their particular sense of vocational calling, given their ability to narrate their responses in light of gospel virtues. We need not make a principled choice between the two. We are free to select one over the other, depending upon the circumstances and how prudent we find one in the given situation.

Similarly, we can see the act of voting within such a matrix of moral meaning: voting is a complex form of social and human communication. As already suggested, we need not construe—and it seems implausible to do so on the grounds of either Western jurisprudence or moral philosophy—voting as some act whereby we become morally culpable for all the deeds of the one for whom we vote. We would do much better to seek to interpret its meaning in light of the cardinal virtues, in light of the gospel, and in light of a shared calling (and thus shared discernment) to bear witness to the alternative politic of the kingdom of God. Justice and courage may sometimes require us to vote; justice and prudence may sometimes require us to abstain, and so forth.

The Myth of Withdrawal

H. Richard Niebuhr's famed work in *Christ and Culture* has done a great deal of disservice to the church.[14] In seeking to relate "Christ" and "culture," he unhelpfully posits a monistic "culture" from which we can stand aside and ask, "How shall we relate to this thing called 'culture'? Shall we withdraw from it? Shall we transform it? Shall we accommodate it?"

But this exhibits a naivete regarding culture that does not provide us with the moral resources we need. Culture is not something we can stand aside from—it is the air we breathe; the water in which we swim; and the language, moral constructs, and social practices in which our very thoughts are formed and our words articulated.

Consequently, our task is not to choose, yet again, some principled and once-chosen-always-followed stance toward culture as such. Instead, we will do much better to practice what I like to call an ad hoc, percipient cultural discernment. We must take each question, issue, and social practice as it comes, on its own terms, seeking to understand deeply what is at stake. With some matters, we will wholeheartedly engage; with some, we will persistently withdraw or object; and with others, we will seek transformation. Moreover, the response that seems consistent with gospel imperatives this decade may not be in the next decade. Because of the persistently perverse and perverting power of sin, a social policy or cultural practice that effected genuine good in one context may show itself oppressive in another.[15]

Consider the following details: Lipscomb claimed that within the three historic Christian options of relating to world powers (Roman Catholic, Protestant, and Anabaptist), the latter approach, which he celebrates, posits "two institutions, the Christian and the worldly," which are "necessarily separate and distinct. That they could form no alliances."[16] But as Donald Durnbaugh has noted in his classic treatment of the Anabaptist or "Believers Church" tradition, the assumption that the two are separate and distinct seems to depend more upon the particularities. The Quakers, for example, held together their pacifism and the calling to govern Pennsylvania. When they were pushed to relent on their pacifism, they refused. In time, they lost status. But when they were asked to help shape the social and political practices of the colony, they did so, upholding their first allegiance.[17] Rather than typify "radicals" as those who "defy civil governments," it would be better to describe them as *those who refuse to compartmentalize the authority and way of Christ.*

In addition, consider the following statement from Lipscomb: "the Christian most effectually promotes public morality by standing aloof from the corrupting influences of worldly institutions."[18] This sort of language proves insufficient in providing concrete guidance. On one hand, it smacks of a concern with self-righteousness that can formulate its own corruption. But more problematic here is that this simply does not work. This is like telling a fish to stay out of the water, like telling a human not to breathe the air. Even Lipscomb himself, as Hicks notes, found it legitimate to take certain jobs within the government, or to make use of the courts for settling differences or collecting debts. Even Stone himself, as noted by Hughes, would find space for a qualified alliance with "human governments" in the abolishment of slavery.

In our own day, such council of "standing aloof" would be even more problematic: banking, local and international business, medical care, immense initiatives of research, and much more besides are integrally and inseparably bound up with "worldly institutions." An ill-conceived notion of aloofness or supposed withdrawal as a primary strategy is not the most fruitful way forward.

Instead of standing aloof, we should embrace a twofold strategy with regard to human agents of civil power. First, call them to accept and embrace the Lordship of Christ, including all the teachings of Jesus regarding forgiveness, reconciliation, and nonviolence.[19] If such an invitation should be rejected, there remains the admonition toward realistic relative goods. Even while we still expect ourselves, faltering as we may be, to practice the way of Christ, and even if the authorities should explicitly reject the Lordship and way of Christ, there still remain relative goods of justice, sharing, mercy, and hospitality—all of which are for the good of the world because they are, we might say, consistent with the grain of the universe, to which we can call the authority.[20] We will likely be able to find all manner of evidence—sociological, psychological, historical—to demonstrate that such gospel practices are for the good of our communities. We then can call the powers that be to take specific steps in the right direction. These steps may not manifest the fullness of Christian confession and conviction, but they may nonetheless contribute to genuine human freedom, beauty, liberation, or compassion.

Vision of the Powers and Power

Lipscomb's counsel might yet be more helpful if we expand our vision of both *power* and *the powers*. There are two particular ways in which I would suggest we qualify or expand Lipscomb's vision here. First, instead of focusing so narrowly upon "civil government," we would do well to expand our vision to consider the many forms and manifestations of the "principalities and powers." As numerous scholars, a century after Lipscomb, have noted, the New Testament is awash in references to the principalities and powers, thrones, dominions, and the like. These powers might be thought of as the sort of thing that is more than the sum of its parts—structures of power that have a sort of "spiritual" reality to them, instantiated in both personal and systemic fashion.

The second but quite important qualification is this: *not* to see "the powers" as inherently or "essentially" or "necessarily" in opposition to the will of God.[21] The structures of power with which the New Testament is so immensely concerned are not innately wicked but created for good, and created under the authority of Christ. Or, at least, this is the stance taken in Colossians 1.[22] We need certain structures, certain mechanisms of power, to facilitate any sort of shared and common life: structures of language, moral norms, mechanisms of exchange, practices of formation, personal and communal boundaries, and the like. These powers are not wicked; they are good. Indeed, all that God has created is "very good."

And yet the powers overreach. They become, as Walter Wink has said, "hell-bent on control."[23] Instead of serving humankind, they oppress, enslave, and become obsessed with their own survival. "Humankind was not made for Sabbath; Sabbath was made for humankind"—this is, in brief, a critique of the fallen (but created for good) powers. Consequently, the question becomes one of redemption rather than destruction.

This reading stands in tension with Fanning and Lipscomb, who speak regularly of the destruction of the powers and the victory of the church.[24] Indeed, 1 Corinthians 15 speaks of the destruction of the powers at the resurrection of the dead. But the context there makes it clear that the powers being destroyed are those that exist as enemies of the Lordship of Christ. Colossians, on the other hand, envisions all the powers being reconciled to the kingdom of God. So we might say that all *rebellious* forms or manifestations of power shall be destroyed, and that all rightful forms and structures of power shall be reconciled to their good, created, and creative intent.

If such a reading is legitimate, then all sorts of ground for fruitful endeavor are opened for us. Consider that the previously presented assertion of Lee Griffith becomes problematic and unhelpful when he

> notes the "widespread misperception of power as a neu-
> tral entity." The debate is not over *how* one uses power

and authority. The concern is *that* one uses power and authority. "In biblical perspective," Griffith counters, "contrary to the modern myth of power as a possession we wield, power possesses us as if it were a creature or a demonic spirit."[25]

Griffith's approach seems highly problematic, given that the biblical narrative envisions every knee bowing and every tongue confessing the Lordship of Christ. The citation from Griffith appears to fail to take into account that the gospel envisions *a power greater than all other powers*—namely, the power of suffering love, truth telling, and obedience to God. The showdown between Pilate and Jesus as recounted in the Gospel of John is telling in this regard: "Do you not know I have the power to kill you?" asks Pilate of Jesus. And even though Pilate exercises that power, the good news of resurrection makes clear that there is a greater power than the preening, self-deluded, imperialist powers of this world.

In addition, an expansive vision of the powers might help us in making more clear a prior point: namely, the uselessness of seeking to "withdraw" from all and every manner of engagement or alliance with the powers. To borrow a quote often mistakenly attributed to Dorothy Day but is nevertheless appropriate here: "We are all caught up in the filthy, rotten system."[26] We obviously would not justify a setting aside of the way of Christ, but we do have to acknowledge the facts. Living between the times, the "system" being inescapable, we are left with the task not of moralistic purity but of finding creative, faithful ways to bear witness to the power of God in Christ, even when we cannot escape all the creeping appendages of said system.

Finally, an expansive vision of the powers might provide us with even more resources for incisive social critique. The

American political Right has been stereotypically suspicious of federal power—and for good reason. But an expansive vision of the powers allows us to pay attention to the idolatry of power in militarism, global capitalism, racism, sexism, and various other systemic forms of hostility. With Lipscomb's narrow view, one might fall prey to a sort of self-righteous withdrawal from "civil government," while failing to take seriously the oppression engendered by global capitalism, monetary policy, and the degradation of the creation. (And it is sometimes the case that these latter ills are fostered by too great a focus on limiting the power of relatively healthy governments.) Would Lipscomb, for example, have been able to better diagnose his own "benign racism," to use Wes Crawford's phrase, if he had seen racism as one of the powers? Expanded in this way, might Lipscomb's considerable capacity for social critique have allowed him to better perceive his own patriarchy and to envision better ways to withdraw from some of the violence of those structures?

There is, of course, much more to say on all these matters. But clearly we have been given a deep and rich exploration of the political theology of David Lipscomb, a resource that can provide us with much wisdom when navigating the hostilities of the world. Living "between the times," let us with Lipscomb continue to bear faithful witness to the kingdom of God and pray for the consummation of all things—that God's will would be done on earth, even as it is in heaven.

NOTES

[1] As Hicks notes, when the *Gospel Advocate* resumed publication following the Civil War, Fanning said that they would seek "to avoid the utterance of a single political thought," even though they were professing and advocating for the Kingdom of God. Fanning, "Suitable Subjects for Discussion in Religious Periodicals," *Gospel Advocate* 8, no. 33 (August 14, 1866): 519.

[2] William Stringfellow, *An Ethic for Christians and Other Aliens in a Strange Land* (Waco: Word, 1973; repr., Eugene, OR: Wipf and Stock, 2004), 13–14.

[3] Barton W. Stone, "A Short History of the Life of Barton W. Stone, Written by Himself" (Cincinnati: J. A. & U. P. James, 1847), in *The Cane Ridge Reader*, ed. Hoke S. Dickinson (n.p., 1972), 27–28.

[4] Joseph Thomas, *The Travels and Gospel Labors of Joseph Thomas* (Winchester, VA: n.p., 1812), 56.

[5] As Hughes noted previously. Cf. "B. W. Stone to Samuel Rennels," Cane Ridge Preservation Project Museum, Cane Ridge, Kentucky, n.d., cited in Newell Williams, "Pursuit of Justice: The Antislavery Pilgrimage of Barton W. Stone," *Encounter* 62, no. 4 (2001): 5.

[6] As Hughes rightly notes in his observation above that "Stone connected his rejection of sectarianism with his rejection of slavery."

[7] Cf. Hicks's previous citation of Lipscomb, "Politics Again," *Gospel Advocate* 18, no. 41 (October 19, 1876): 1008–13. Also note the argument made by former war journalist and now pastor Chris Hedges, *War Is a Force That Gives Us Meaning* (New York: Public Affairs, [2002] 2014), 3, who describes the intoxicating manner of war.

[8] Lipscomb, "Babylon," *Gospel Advocate* 33, no. 22 (June 2, 1881): 340.

[9] And we should note that one publicly challenges those liturgies only to one's own detriment.

[10] George Creed, *How We Advertised America; the First Telling of the Amazing Story of the Committee on Public Information That Carried the Gospel of Americanism to Every Corner of the Globe* (New York: Harper & Brothers, 1920).

[11] Lipscomb, *Civil Government: Its Origin, Mission, and Destiny, and the Christian's Relation to It* (Nashville: McQuiddy Printing Company, 1913), v.

[12] As one contemporary example of such an approach, see Ted Lewis, ed., *Electing Note to Vote: Christian Reflections on Reasons for Not Voting* (Eugene, OR: Wipf and Stock, 2008).

[13] See Hicks's previous citation of Lipscomb: "God has forbidden his servants to add anything to the things he has ordained" (Lipscomb, "Can Christians Vote and Hold Office? Rejoinder I," *Gospel Advocate* 23, no. 1 [January 6, 1881]: 3).

[14] H. Richard Niebuhr, *Christ and Culture* (New York: Harper & Row, 1975).

[15] One fascinating example in Lipscomb's context was the Temperance movement; see the prior discussion.

[16] Lipscomb, "The Church of Christ and World-Powers," *Gospel Advocate* 8, no. 2 (January 9, 1866): 28–30.

[17] Donald Durnbaugh, *The Believers' Church: The History and Character of Radical Protestantism* (Scottdale, PA: Herald Press, 1985), chapter 10.

[18] Lipscomb, *Civil Government*, 147.

[19] My "first" here is not necessarily a chronological first but a "first" of importance. Prudence and strategy are legitimate for Christians: "be ye wise as serpents, and harmless as doves."

[20] Even practices of nonviolence may be advocated as good news, even if someone rejects the Lordship of Christ. There has been increasing study of the social and political efficacy of nonviolence in service to particular forms of freedom and justice. As just one fascinating recent example, see Srdja Popovic, *Blueprint for Revolution: How to Use Rice Pudding, Lego Men, and Other Nonviolent Techniques to Galvanize Communities, Overthrow Dictators, or Simply Change the World* (New York: Spiegel & Grau, 2015).

[21] Lipscomb, "Questions for the Editor," *Gospel Advocate* 10, no. 2 (January 14, 1869): 30; and Lipscomb, "Church of Christ and World-Powers, No. 6," *Gospel Advocate* 8, no. 10 (March 6, 1866): 146, both cited herein: "the two are essentially antagonistic," and "*they must forever remain distinct.*"

[22] Here I am drawing off the reading of the powers done so extensively by Walter Wink.

[23] Walter Wink, *Engaging the Powers: Discernment and Resistance in a World of Domination* (Minneapolis: Fortress, 1992), 49.

[24] See Hicks's summary of Fanning.

[25] I wonder, instead, whether Griffith here does not betray his own modernist tendencies, in which "autonomy," as the great hallmark of being a moral actor, must distance itself from the power or authority of others. If, instead, we focus upon a sort of hermeneutic grounded in narrative that is in conversation with virtue traditions, we find that rightful authority is a necessary construct to any sort of moral life. Similarly, Dorothy Day famously made it clear that she was in subjection (rightfully, as she saw it) to the bishops and the authority of the church.

[26] Brian Terrell, "Dorthy Day's 'filthy, rotten system' likely wasn't hers at all," *National Catholic Reporter* (April 16, 2012), accessed November 7, 2019, https://www.ncronline.org/news/people/dorothy-days-filthy-rotten-system-likely-wasnt-hers-all?_ga=2.118434318.626697426.1561493436-1232479879.1561493436.

A Chronological Bibliography of and about David Lipscomb

JOHN MARK HICKS

Works by David Lipscomb

The Religious Sentiment, Its Social and Political Influence: An Address before the Alumni Society of Franklin College, Tenn., Delivered on the 4th of July, 1855. Nashville: Cameron & Fall, 1855. Available at https://webfiles.acu .edu/departments/Library/HR/restmov_nov11/www.mun.ca/rels /restmov/texts/dlipscomb/1855.html.

Gospel Advocate. Lipscomb edited and contributed to this journal from 1866 until his death in 1917, though the last few years he was unable to actively participate in editorial activities.

Offerings to the Lord: A Tract. Nashville: Lipscomb & Sewell, 1878.

The Standard and the Hymn-Book, with An Exposition of Its Course toward the Missionary Society. Nashville: A. M. Sewell, 1883.

Difficulties in Religion Considered (1885). In *Salvation from Sin,* ed. James Walton Shepherd, 347–64. Nashville: McQuiddy Printing Company, 1913.

Civil Government: Its Origin, Mission, and Destiny, and the Christian's Relation to It. Nashville: Gospel Advocate Publishing Company, 1889. Reprinted by McQuiddy Printing Company, Nashville, 1913. Reprinted by Gospel Advocate Company, Nashville, 1957. Reprinted by Vance Publications, Pensacola, 2006. Available at https://webfiles.acu.edu /departments/Library/HR/restmov_nov11/www.mun.ca/rels/restmov /texts/dlipscomb/civgov.html.

My work is deeply indebted to McGarvey Ice, who published a bibliography on his website, which is accessible here: https://mcgarveyice.wordpress.com/2017/11/09/david -lipscomb-a-bibliography/ (accessed March 5, 2019). I have edited and added to his list but the substance is his, though I am responsible for this final form and its limitations.

Christian Unity: How Promoted, How Destroyed. Faith and Opinion.
Nashville: Gospel Advocate Publishing Company, 1891. Reprinted by
McQuiddy Printing Company, Nashville, 1916. Reprinted under a short
title, *On Christian Unity*, by Doulos Christou Press, Indianapolis, 2006.
Available at https://webfiles.acu.edu/departments/library/hr/restmov
_nov11/www.mun.ca/rels/restmov/texts/dlipscomb/cufo/cufooa.htm.

*Life and Sermons of Jesse L. Sewell: An Account of His Life, Labors and
Character.* Nashville: Gospel Advocate Publishing Company, 1891.
Second and third editions, actually printings, released in 1891 by Gospel
Advocate Publishing Company, Nashville. Fourth edition by Gospel
Advocate Company, Nashville, 1954.

"Introduction." In *Texas Poems*, ed. Ida Van Zandt Jarvis, 3. Nashville:
Gospel Advocate Publishing Company, 1893.

Notes on the International S. S. Lessons for 1895. Nashville: Gospel Advocate
Publishing Company, 1895.

*A Commentary on the Acts of the Apostles, with Questions Suited for the
Use of Families and Schools.* Nashville: Gospel Advocate Publishing
Company, 1896. Printed at least four times, one perhaps as late as 1939.

Notes on the International S. S. Lessons for 1896. Nashville: Gospel Advocate
Publishing Company, 1896.

"Man: His Beginning, Training, and End." In *Biographies and Sermons, A
Collection of Original Sermons by Different Men, with a Biographical
Sketch of Each Man Accompanying His Sermon, Illustrated by Half-Tone
Cuts*, ed. F. D. Srygley. Nashville: Gospel Advocate Publishing Company,
1898. Reprinted by Gospel Advocate Company, Nashville, 1961, 165–84.

"Introduction." In *Instrumental Music in the Worship: A Discussion between H.
L. Calhoun and M. C. Kurfees, with an Appendix. Introduction by David
Lipscomb, Editor of the* Gospel Advocate, ed. H. L. Calhoun and M. C.
Kurfees, 1–6. Nashville: Gospel Advocate Publishing Company, 1901.

*Instruments of Music in the Service of God: An Examination of the Subject
from the Teaching of Both the Old and the New Testaments.* Nashville:
McQuiddy Printing Company, 1903.

"Address." In *Franklin College and Its Influence*, ed. James E. Scobey.
Nashville: McQuiddy Printing Company, 1906. Reprinted by Gospel
Advocate Company, Nashville, 1954, 358–63.

"Notice of the Death of William Anderson." In *Franklin College and Its
Influence*, ed. James E. Scobey. Nashville: McQuiddy Printing Company,
1906. Reprinted by Gospel Advocate Company, Nashville, 1954, 443–47.

"Tolbert Fanning's Teaching and Influence." In *Franklin College and Its
Influence*, ed. James E. Scobey. Nashville: McQuiddy Printing Company,
1906. Reprinted by Gospel Advocate Company, Nashville, 1954, 7–111.

Queries and Answers by David Lipscomb, Editor of the Gospel Advocate, ed. James Walton Shepherd. Nashville: McQuiddy Printing Company, 1910. Second and third editions in 1910 and 1911, respectively, both by McQuiddy Printing Company, Nashville. Fourth and fifth editions in 1918 and 1942, respectively, by F. L. Rowe, Cincinnati. Sixth edition by Gospel Advocate Company, Nashville, 1963. As editor, Shepherd freely adapted Lipscomb's work for the sake of clarity and coherence.

The Sabbath: Which Day Shall We Observe—The First or the Seventh? Nashville: Gospel Advocate Publishing Company and/or McQuiddy Printing Company, prior to 1910.

Salvation from Sin by David Lipscomb, Editor of the Gospel Advocate, ed. J. W. Shepherd. Nashville: McQuiddy Printing Company, 1913. Second edition by Gospel Advocate Company, Nashville, 1950. Reprinted by Faith and Facts, Indianapolis, ca. 1995. As editor, Shepherd freely adapted Lipscomb's work for the sake of clarity and coherence.

Contributor. *Christian Treasures, An Exposition of Vital Themes by Earnest and Forceful Writers.* Volume 1, ed. A. B. Lipscomb. Nashville: McQuiddy Printing Company, 1916.

Contributor. *Christian Treasures, An Exposition of Vital Themes by Earnest and Forceful Writers.* Volume 2, ed. A. B. Lipscomb. Nashville: McQuiddy Printing Company, 1916.

Queries and Answers by Lipscomb and Sewell Being a Compilation of Queries with Answers by D. Lipscomb and E. G. Sewell, Covering a Period of Forty Years of Their Joint Editorial Labors on the Gospel Advocate, ed. M. C. Kurfees. Nashville: McQuiddy Printing Company, 1921. Second printing changed to *Questions Answered by Lipscomb and Sewell* . . . . Reprinted by McQuiddy Printing Company, Nashville, 1952 and 1957, and by Gospel Advocate Company, Nashville, in 1963 and 1974.

A Commentary on the New Testament Epistles by David Lipscomb. Volume I: *Romans,* ed. J. W. Shepherd. Nashville: Gospel Advocate Company, 1933. As editor, Shepherd freely adapted Lipscomb's work for the sake of clarity and coherence.

A Commentary on the New Testament Epistles by David Lipscomb. Volume II: *First Corinthians,* ed. J. W. Shepherd. Nashville: Gospel Advocate Company, 1935. As editor, Shepherd freely adapted Lipscomb's work for the sake of clarity and coherence.

A Commentary on the New Testament Epistles by David Lipscomb. Volume III: *Second Corinthians and Galatians,* ed. J. W. Shepherd. Nashville: Gospel Advocate Company, 1936. As editor, Shepherd freely adapted Lipscomb's work for the sake of clarity and coherence.

A Commentary on the Gospel by John, ed. C. E. W. Dorris. Nashville: Gospel Advocate Company, 1939.

A Commentary on the New Testament Epistles by David Lipscomb. Volume IV: *Ephesians, Philippians and Colossians*, ed. J. W. Shepherd. Nashville: Gospel Advocate Company, 1939. As editor, Shepherd freely adapted Lipscomb's work for the sake of clarity and coherence.

A Commentary on the New Testament Epistles by David Lipscomb. Volume V: *I, II Thessalonians, I, II Timothy, Titus, and Philemon*, ed. J. W. Shepherd. Nashville: Gospel Advocate Company, 1942. As editor, Shepherd freely adapted Lipscomb's work for the sake of clarity and coherence.

A Commentary on the New Testament Epistles by David Lipscomb. Volume I: *Romans*, ed. J. W. Shepherd. Second ed. rev. and enl. Nashville: Gospel Advocate Company, 1943. As editor, Shepherd freely adapted Lipscomb's work for the sake of clarity and coherence.

Works about David Lipscomb

Srygley, F. D. "Life of David Lipscomb." In *Biographies and Sermons, A Collection of Original Sermons by Different Men, with a Biographical Sketch of Each Man Accompanying His Sermon, Illustrated by Half-Tone Cuts*. Nashville: Gospel Advocate Publishing Company, 1898. Reprinted by Gospel Advocate Company, Nashville, 1961, 150–64.

"David Lipscomb Memorial Number," *Gospel Advocate* 59, no. 49 (December 6, 1917): 1169–88.

Boles, H. Leo. *Biographical Sketches of Gospel Preachers, Including the Pioneer Preachers of the Restoration Movement and Many Other Preachers through Decades down to the Present Generation Who Have Passed to Their Reward*. Nashville: Gospel Advocate Company, 1932.

Lipscomb, Granvile Quartus. *David Lipscomb: Lineage, Student, Farmer, Preacher, Writer, Teacher, Christian, Uncle*. Unpublished, in the possession of Lipscomb University, 1938.

Lewis, John Thomas. *The Christian and the Government: Or, A Review of the Bible Banner's Position on Christians Going to War*. Birmingham: Lewis, 1945.

West, Earl Irvin. *The Life and Times of David Lipscomb*. Henderson: Religious Book Service, 1954.

Barnett, Herman L. "David Lipscomb's Doctrine of the Church." Master's thesis, Butler University, 1956.

Vaughn, J. Roy, "David Lipscomb." In *The Gospel Advocate Centennial Volume*, ed. B. C. Goodpasture, 14–44. Nashville: Gospel Advocate Company, 1956.

Harrell, David Edwin, Jr. "Disciples of Christ Pacifism in Nineteenth Century Tennessee." *Tennessee Historical Quarterly* 21, no. 3 (1962): 263–74.

Holland, Tom. *David Lipscomb: An Example of Ethical Power in Preaching.* Master's thesis, Abilene Christian College, 1964.

Hooper, Robert E. *The Political and Educational Ideas of David Lipscomb.* PhD dissertation, George Peabody College for Teachers, 1965.

Campbell, Thomas L. *The Contribution of David Lipscomb and the Gospel Advocate to Religious Education in the Churches of Christ. Or, David Lipscomb's Contribution to the Restoration Movement.* PhD dissertation, Southern Baptist Theological Seminary, 1968.

Wallace, Foy E., Jr. *The Christian and Civil Government: With Review of Lipscomb's Theory of Civil Government, by O. C. Lambert.* Nashville: Foy E. Wallace Jr. Publications, 1968.

Robinson, John Louis. *David Lipscomb: Journalist in Texas, 1872.* Quanah, TX: Nortex, 1973.

Murrell, Arthur V. "David Lipscomb: Moderate in the Middle; or David Lipscomb Reconsidered." *Discipliana* 34, no. 4 (Winter 1974): 43–57.

Harrell, David Edwin. "From Consent to Dissent: The Emergence of the Churches of Christ in America." *Restoration Quarterly* 19, no. 2 (1976): 98–111.

Seawright, Sandy. "Ten 'Greatest Tennesseans'—A Reappraisal." *Tennessee Historical Quarterly* 35, no. 2 (Summer 1976): 222–24.

Hooper, Robert E. *A Call to Remember: Chapters in Nashville Restoration History.* Nashville: Gospel Advocate Company, 1977.

Robinson, John L. "David Lipscomb in Texas." *Restoration Quarterly* 21, no. 1 (1978): 26–32.

Hooper, Robert E. *Crying in the Wilderness: A Biography of David Lipscomb.* Nashville: David Lipscomb College, 1979.

Woodson, William. *Standing for their Faith: A History of Churches of Christ in Tennessee, 1900–1950.* Henderson, TN: J & W Publications, 1979.

West, Earl Irvin. "James A. Harding." *Restoration Quarterly* 24, no. 2 (1981): 65–79.

Hooper, Robert E. "The Lipscomb Family." In *Nashville Families and Homes, Paragraphs from Nashville History Lecture Series 1979–1981,* 90–103. Nashville: The Nashville Room, The Public Library of Nashville & Davidson County, 1983.

Haymes, Don. "Hall Calhoun and His 'Nashville Brethren,' 1897–1935." *Restoration Quarterly* 27, no. 1 (1984): 37–48.

Foster, Douglas A. *The Struggle for Unity during the Period of Division of the Restoration Movement, 1875–1900.* PhD dissertation, Vanderbilt University, 1987.

Dunnavant, Anthony L. "David Lipscomb on the Church and the Poor." *Restoration Quarterly,* 33, no. 2 (1991): 75–85.

Woodson, William, and J. E. Choate. *Sounding Brass and Clanging Cymbals: The History and Significance of Instrumental Music in the Restoration Movement (1827–1968).* Henderson, TN: Freed-Hardeman University, 1991.

Dunnavant, Anthony L. "David Lipscomb and the 'Preferential Option for the Poor' among Post-Bellum Churches of Christ." In *Poverty and Ecclesiology: Nineteenth-Century Evangelicals in the Light of Liberation Theology,* ed. Justo L. Gonzalez and Anthony L. Dunnavant, 27–50. Collegeville, MN: Liturgical Press, 1992.

Hughes, Richard T. "The Apocalyptic Origins of Churches of Christ and the Triumph of Modernism." *Religion and American Culture: A Journal of Interpretation* 2, no. 2 (1992): 181–214.

Elrod, Mark A. *Churches of Christ and the "War Question": The Influence of Christian Journals.* PhD dissertation, Vanderbilt University, 1995.

Allen, C. Leonard. "Silena Moore Holman (1850–1915), Voice of the 'New Woman' among Churches of Christ." *Discipliana* 56, no. 1 (1996): 3–11.

Hughes, Richard T. *Reviving the Ancient Faith: The Story of Churches of Christ in America.* Grand Rapids, MI: Eerdmans, 1996. Reprint, Abilene Christian University Press, Abilene, TX, 2008.

Brewster, Ben. "Torn Asunder the Civil War, David Lipscomb, and the 1906 Division of the Disciples." Master's thesis, Cincinnati Bible College & Seminary, 1999.

Casey, Michael W., "Pacifism and Nonviolence: The Prophetic Voice of the African American Churches of Christ." *Discipliana* 69, no. 2 (1999): 35–49.

Foster, Douglas A. "Churches of Christ and Baptism: An Historical and Theological Overview." *Restoration Quarterly,* 43, no. 2 (2001): 79–94.

Olbricht, Thomas H., "The Peace Heritage of the Churches of Christ." In *The Fragmentation of the Church and Its Unity in Peacemaking,* ed. John D. Rempel and Jeffrey Gros, 196–219. Grand Rapids, MI: Eerdmans, 2001.

Roberts, R. L. "Lipscomb, David." In *The Churches of Christ,* ed. Richard T. Hughes and R. L. Roberts, 252–53. Denominations in America, 10. Henry Warner Bowden, Series Ed. Westport: Greenwood Press, 2001.

Casey, Michael W. "From Religious Outsiders to Insiders: The Rise and Fall of Pacifism in the Churches of Christ." *Journal of Church and State* 44, no. 3 (2002): 455–75.

Hall, Gary H. "A Critique of the Place of the Old Testament in the Early Historical Perspective of the Stone-Campbell Movement: Campbell through Lipscomb." *Stone-Campbell Journal* 5, no. 1 (2002): 25–47.

Keech, Kevin P. *David Lipscomb's "Apocalyptic" Worldview: A Partial Critique of Richard Hughes's Stone-Campbell Historiography.* Master's thesis, Harding School of Theology, 2002.

Little, David L. "The Aversion to Biblical Interpretation in the Thought of David Lipscomb and Tolbert Fanning." *Restoration Quarterly* 44, no. 3 (2002): 159–64.

Hooper, Robert E. "Lipscomb, David (1831–1917)." In *Encyclopedia of the Stone-Campbell Movement*, ed. Douglas A. Foster, Paul M. Blowers, Anthony L. Dunnavant, and Newell Williams, 480–82. Grand Rapids, MI: Eerdmans, 2004.

Hicks, John Mark, "Theodicy in Early Stone-Campbell Perspectives." In *Restoring the First-Century Church in the Twenty-First Century: Essays on the Stone-Campbell Restoration Movement in Honor of Don Hayme*, ed. Warren Lewis and Hans Rollmann, 287–303. Eugene, OR: Wipf and Stock Publishers, 2005.

Foster, Douglas A. "The 1906 Census of Religious Bodies and Division in the Stone-Campbell Movement: A Closer Look." *Discipliana* 66, no. 3 (2006): 83–93.

Hicks, John Mark, and Bobby Valentine. *Kingdom Come: Embracing the Spiritual Legacy of David Lipscomb and James Harding.* Abilene, TX: Leafwood Publishers, 2006.

Sringham, Edward P. *The Radical Libertarian Political Economy of 19th Century Preacher David Lipscomb.* The Independent Institute Working Paper Number 66, 2006, available at http://www.independent.org/pdf /working_papers/66_radical.pdf. Also at the Mercatus Center of George Mason University (April 2009), available at https://www .mercatus.org/system/files/Radical_Libertarian_Political_Economy_of _David_Lipscomb_by_Stringham.pdf.

Mayden, Brandon K. *The Role of the Restoration Movement Editors Concerning the Use of Instrumental Music in Worship: 1866–1906.* Master's thesis, Cincinnati Christian University, 2007.

Olbricht, Thomas H. "The Theology of the Church in Churches of Christ." *Restoration Quarterly* 50, no. 1 (2008): 15–34.

Valentine, Bobby. "Lipscomb of Texas vs. Lipscomb of Nashville: R. L. Whiteside's Rejection of David Lipscomb's Pacifism." In *And the Word*

Became Flesh: Studies in History, Communication and Scripture in Memory of Michael W. Casey, ed. Thomas H. Olbricht and David Fleer, 124–39. Eugene, OR: Pickwick Publishers, 2009.

Mead, Jason. "An Abandonment of the Christian Religion: War, Politics, and Society in the Writings of Tolbert Fanning and David Lipscomb, 1855–1876." *Journal of East Tennessee History* 82 (2010): 33–52.

Hooper, Robert E. *Crying in the Wilderness: The Life and Influence of David Lipscomb*. Revised edition. Nashville: Lipscomb University, 2011.

Anguish, Jeremy. "David Lipscomb's Vision of Unity through Purity." Guided research paper, Harding School of Theology, 2012.

Grubbs, Shaun. *The Heritage of Pacifism in the Stone-Campbell Movement: A General Study*. Master's thesis, Abilene Christian University, 2012.

Hicks, John Mark. "David Lipscomb on the Urban Poor." *Missio Dei: A Journal of Missional Theology and Praxis* 3, no. 2 (August 2012). Available at http://missiodeijournal.com/issues/md-3-2/authors /md-3-2-hicks.

Brown, Joel A. "Concern for the Poor in the Nashville Bible School Tradition: David Lipscomb and James A. Harding." *Restoration Quarterly* 55, no. 2 (2013): 91–106.

Vance, Laurence. "Alexander Campbell, Tolbert Fanning, David Lipscomb: A Nineteenth-Century Anti-War Triumvirate." Libertarian Christian Institute (March 2013). Available at https://libertarianchristians.com /2013/03/29/campbell-fanning-lipscomb-anti-war/.

Casey, Brian. *Subjects of the Kingdom: Christians, Conscience, Government, and the Reign of the King*. Atchison, KS: Encounter Music and Creative Sources, 2016.

Goode, Richard C. "The Calling of Crappy Citizenship: A Plea for Christian Anarchy." *The Other Journal: An Intersection of Theology and Culture* 30 (November 1, 2018). Available at https://theotherjournal .com/2018/11/01/the-calling-of-crappy-citizenship-a-plea-for-christian -anarchy/?fbclid=IwAR2nHprdAquZXpEcROQKpwEQdiB_04hL_Vcw5 _O_NOXq58zLnQkg1nc_AJI.

Ice, McGarvey. "David Lipscomb on Rebaptism: Contexts of a Controversy." *Restoration Quarterly* 60, no. 3 (2018): 129–46.

Contributors

Lee C. Camp is a professor of theology and ethics at Lipscomb University in Nashville, Tennessee. He is most recently the author of *Scandalous Witness: A Little Political Manifesto for Christians*, and is host and executive producer of *Tokens Show*, the world's only long-running theological variety show. He is married to Laura and has three sons. For more, visit www.tokensshow.com or www.leeccamp.com.

Richard C. Goode is a professor of history at Lipscomb University in Nashville, Tennessee, where he has taught for twenty-nine years. His research has covered such topics as the history of the Vanderbilt Divinity School and the political theology of Will D. Campbell. He was also the founding director of the Lipscomb Initiative for Education (LIFE) program, which offers higher education in Nashville-area prisons. He and his wife, Candyee, have two married daughters.

John Mark Hicks is a professor of theology at Lipscomb University in Nashville, Tennessee. He has taught for thirty-eight years in schools associated with the Churches of Christ. He has published fifteen books as well as many academic and popular articles, lectured in twenty countries and forty states, and is married to Jennifer. They share five living children and six grandchildren.

Richard T. Hughes is Scholar in Residence in the College of Bible and Ministry at Lipscomb University. Over the course of an almost fifty-year career, Hughes has taught and published on the role of Christian primitivism in American culture, on the intersection of Christian faith and the life of the mind, on the role of race in American history and life, on the meaning of Christian nationalism, and on the history of Churches of Christ. He delights in team-teaching with his wife, Jan, an honors first-year seminar at Lipscomb on the theme "Learning to Tell Our Stories."

Joshua Ward Jeffery is the chair of the Department of Humanities and a US history teacher at The Orme School, Mayer, Arizona. Jeffery holds an MA in US history from the University of Tennessee, and an MTS with specializations in American religious history and political theology from Vanderbilt University. His research focuses on religion, politics, and war in American history. He is happily married to Candace, and they have two black dogs.